PRACTICAL HANDBOOK
FEEDING YOUR TODDLER

PRACTICAL HANDBOOK

FEEDING YOUR
TODDLER

How to give your growing child the best of health and vitality

SARA LEWIS

LORENZ BOOKS

This edition published by Lorenz Books in 2002

© Anness Publishing Limited 1996, 2002

Published in the USA by Lorenz Books
Anness Publishing Inc.
27 West 20th Street
New York
NY 10011

Lorenz Books is an imprint of Anness Publishing Inc.

www.lorenzbooks.com

All rights reserved. No part of this publication may be reproduced, stored in a retrieval system, or transmitted in any way or by any means, electronic, mechanical, photocopying, recording or otherwise, without the prior written permission of the copyright holder.

A CIP catalogue record for this book is available from the British Library.

Publisher: Joanna Lorenz
Project Editors: Judith Simons and Emma Wish
Designer: Sue Storey
Special Photography: John Freeman
Stylist: Judy Williams
Home Economists: Sara Lewis and Petra Jackson

Previously published as *What to Feed Your Toddler*,
and as part of a larger compendium, *Cooking for Babies and Toddlers*

1 3 5 7 9 10 8 6 4 2

NOTES
Standard spoon and cup measures are level.
Large eggs are used unless otherwise stated.

PICTURE CREDITS
The publishers would like to thank the following
for additional images used in this book:

Key: t = top; b = bottom; l = left; r = right.

Bubbles: page 11 br (Jacqui Farrow); pages 9t, 10t (Ian West)
Reflections/Jenny Woodcock: pages 11br, 19, 48, 78

Contents

Introduction	6
Lunch Specials	14
Going Green	32
Quick Teas	42
Toast Toppers	58
Easy Peasy Puds	68
Quick Cakes and Bakes the Kids Can Make	80
Index	94
Acknowledgements	96

INTRODUCTION

Once your child has reached 12 months he or she will be enjoying a varied diet and eating habits and their personal food preferences will be developing. It is now vitally important to lay the foundations of a good and well balanced eating regime.

This is a time when food fads may also develop. Try to weather this period of fussy eating – all children will experience it at some time, and even good eaters will go through a picky stage. Hopefully the fad will go as quickly as it comes, but while it lasts mealtimes can become a nightmare.

A Balanced and Varied Diet

Give your child a selection of foods in the four main food groups daily:

Cereal and filler foods: include three to four helpings of the following per day – breakfast cereals, bread, pasta, potatoes, rice.

Fruit and vegetables: try to have three or four helpings per day. Choose from fresh, canned, frozen or dried.

Meat and/or alternatives: one to two portions per day – meat – all kinds, including burgers and sausages, poultry, fish (fresh, canned or frozen), eggs (well-cooked), lentils and pulses (for example baked beans, red kidney beans, chick-peas), finely chopped nuts, smooth peanut butter, seeds, tofu, and Quorn.

Dairy foods: include 1 pint of milk per day or a mix of milk, cheese, yogurt and fromage frais. For a child who goes off drinking milk, try flavouring it or using it in custards, ice cream, rice pudding or cheese sauce. A carton of yogurt or 40g/ 1½oz of cheese have the same amount of calcium as 190ml/⅓ pint of milk.

THE IMPORTANCE OF BREAKFAST

Breakfast is a vitally important start for any young child. Count back: your child may have had tea at 5 o'clock the previous day and if she misses breakfast at 8 o'clock she will not have eaten for 15 hours. Allow time to sit down and don't hurry your child. Offer milk and cereals, orange juice diluted with a little water (not squash), a few slices of fruit and half a piece of toast preferably spread with smooth peanut butter or Marmite.

Above: *Cereal and filler foods, like bread, pasta and rice.*

Above: *Fruit and vegetables, including frozen, dried and canned goods.*

Above: *Meat and meat alternatives, like pulses and nuts.*

Above: *Dairy foods such as milk, cheese and yogurt.*

Marmite toast

Sliced pears

FATS

As adults we are all aware of the need to cut down on our fat consumption, but when eating together as a family, bear in mind that fat is a useful source of energy in a child's diet. The energy from fat is in concentrated form, so that your child can take in the calories she needs for growth and development before her stomach becomes overfull. Fat in food is also a valuable source of the fat-soluble vitamins, A, D, E and K, as well as essential fatty acids that the body cannot make by itself.

In general, fat is best provided by foods which contain not just fat but other essential nutrients as well, such as dairy products, eggs, meat and fish. Whole milk and its products such as cheese and yogurt, and eggs contain the fat-soluble vitamins A and D, while sunflower oil, nuts and oily fish are a good source of various essential fatty acids.

It is wise to cut down on deep frying and to grill or oven bake foods where possible. All children love chips and crisps but do keep them as a treat rather than a daily snack.

FRUIT AND VEGETABLES

Fresh fruit and vegetables play an essential part in a balanced diet. Offer fresh fruit, such as slices of apple or banana, for breakfast and tea, and perhaps thin sticks of raw carrot and celery for lunch. Instead of biscuits and crisps, offer your child raisins, ready-to-eat apricots, satsumas or carrots and apple slices if she wants a mid-morning or afternoon snack. Keep the fruit bowl within easy reach so your child may be tempted to pick up a banana as she walks through the kitchen.

Above: *A good mixture of the four basic food types will provide maximum energy and vitality for growing children.*

SNACKS

Young children cannot eat enough food at mealtimes to meet their needs for energy and growth and snacks can play a vital part in meeting these needs. However keep chocolate biscuits and crisps as a treat. They contain little goodness and are bad for the teeth. At meal times keep sweets out of sight until the main course has been eaten.

Above: *Do keep sweets and chocolate as treats – give fruit and vegetables as day-to-day snacks.*

Bread sticks

Courgettes

Melon

Broccoli

Sultanas

Raisins

Dried apricots

Coping With a Fussy Eater

We all have different sized appetites whatever our age, and young children are no exception. Children's appetites fluctuate greatly and often tail off just before a growth spurt. All children go through food fads; some just seem to last longer and be more difficult than others.

A toddler's appetite varies enormously and you may find that she will eat very well one day and eat hardly anything the next. Be guided by your toddler and try to think in terms of what the child has eaten over several days rather than just concentrating on one day.

At the time, it can be really frustrating and worrying. Try not to think of the food that you have just thrown away but try to think more in the long term. Jot down the foods that your child has actually eaten over three or four days or up to a week. You may actually be surprised, it's not just yogurts and crisps after all!

Once you have a list you may find a link between the foods your child eats and the time of day. Perhaps your child eats better when eating with the family, or when the house is quiet. If you do find a link then build on it. You might find that your child is snacking on chocolate, doughnuts, soft drinks or chips when out with friends, and that fussiness at home is really a full tummy. Or it may be that by cutting out a milky drink and a biscuit mid-morning and offering a sliced apple instead, your child may not be so full up come lunch time. Perhaps you could hide the biscuit tin once visitors have had one, so that tiny hands can't keep reaching for more.

If your toddler seems hungrier at breakfast then you could offer eggy bread, a grilled sausage or a few banana slices with her cereal.

Above: *Don't panic about food rejection. Be patient and keep a journal listing what your child actually does eat.*

Right: *Fresh, healthy snacks will preserve the appetite for main meals.*

Although this all sounds obvious, when rushing about caring for a toddler and perhaps an older child or new baby, life becomes rather blurred and it can be difficult to stand back and look at things objectively.

REFUSING TO EAT
A child will always eat if she is hungry although it may not be when you want her to eat. A child can stay fit and healthy on surprisingly little. Providing your child is growing and gaining weight then don't fuss, but if you are worried, talk to your health visitor or doctor. Take the lead from your child, never force feed a child and try not to let meal times become a battle ground.

MAKING MEAL TIMES FUN

Coping with a fussy eater can be incredibly frustrating. The less she eats the crosser you get and so the spiral goes on as your toddler learns how to control meal times. To break this vicious circle, try diffusing things by involving your child in the preparation of the meal. You could pack up a picnic with your child's help, choosing together what to take. Then go somewhere different to eat, it could be the back garden, the swings or even the car. Alternatively, have a dollies' or teddies' tea party or make a camp under the dining table or even in the cupboard under the stairs.

Even very young children enjoy having friends for tea. If your child is going through a fussy or non-eating stage, invite over a little friend with a good appetite. Try to take a back seat and don't make a fuss over how much the visiting child eats.

Above: *Changing the scene and breaking routine can help a lot.*

Below: *Making the meal a special event can distract the child from any eating worries.*

Above: *Getting your child to help you cook the food will encourage them to eat it, too.*

Above: *Children are more likely to eat with friends of their own age around them.*

10 TIPS TO COPE WITH A FUSSY EATER

1 Try to find meals that the rest of the family enjoys and where there are at least one or two things the fussy child will eat as well. It may seem easier to cook only foods that your child will eat but it means a very limited diet for everyone else and your child will never get the chance to have a change of mind and try something new.

2 Serve smaller portions of food to your child.

3 Invite round her friend with a hearty appetite. A good example sometimes works but don't comment on how much the visiting child has eaten.

4 Invite an adult who the child likes for supper – a granny, uncle or friend. Sometimes a child will eat for someone else without any fuss at all.

5 Never force feed a child.

6 If your child is just playing with the food and won't eat, quietly remove the plate without fuss and don't offer pudding.

7 Try to make meal times enjoyable and talk about what the family has been doing.

8 Try limiting snacks and drinks between meals so your child feels hungrier when it comes to family meal times. Alternatively, offer more nutritious snacks and smaller main meals if your child eats better that way.

9 Offer drinks after a meal so that they don't spoil the appetite.

10 Offer new foods when you know your child is hungry and hopefully more receptive.

Above: *Remember to give drinks after the meal, not before.*

EATING TOGETHER

Eating together as a family should be a happy part of the day, but can turn into a nightmare if everyone is tired or you feel as though the only things your children will eat are chips.

There is nothing worse than preparing a lovely supper, laying the table and sitting down with everyone and then one child refuses to eat, shrieks her disapproval or just pushes the food around the plate. However hard you try to ignore this behaviour, the meal is spoilt for everyone, especially if this is a regular occurrence. It's not fair on you or anyone else.

If you feel this is just a passing phase, then you could try just ignoring it and carry on regardless. Try to praise the good things, perhaps the way the child sits nicely at the table or the way she holds a knife and fork. Talk about the things that have been happening in the day, rather than concentrating on the meal itself. Try to avoid comparing your child's appetite with more hearty eaters. With luck, this particular fad will go away.

However, if it becomes a regular thing and mealtimes always seem more like a battleground than a happy family gathering, perhaps it's time for a sterner approach.

First steps

• Check to see if there is something physically wrong with your child. Has she been ill? If she has, she may not have recovered fully. If you're worried, then ask your doctor.
• Perhaps your child has enlarged adenoids or tonsils which could make swallowing difficult, or perhaps she has a food allergy, such as coeliacs disease – an intolerance to gluten – which may be undiagnosed but which would give the child tummy pains after eating. Again, check with your doctor.
• Is your child worried or stressed? If your family circumstances have changed – a new baby perhaps, or if you've moved recently – your child may be unhappy or confused.
• Is your child trying to get your attention?

Above: *Good seating of the right height will contribute to comfort and relaxation.*

Secondly

Look at the way in which you as a family eat. Do you eat at regular times? Do you sit down to eat or catch snacks on the move? Do you enjoy your food or do you always feel rushed and harassed? Children will pick up habits from their parents – bad as well as good. If you don't tend to sit down to a meal or you have the habit of getting up during meal times to do other jobs, then it's hard to expect the child to behave differently.

Finally

Talk things over with all the family. If you all feel enough is enough, then it's time to make a plan of action. Explain that from now on you are all going to eat together where possible, when and where you say so. You will choose the food, there will be three meals a day and no snacks. Since milk is filling and dulls the appetite, milky drinks will only be given after a meal; during the meal water or juice will be provided.

It is vitally important to involve all the family in this strategy so that there is no dipping into the biscuit tin or raiding the cupboard for crisps after school. Make sure that the fussy eater is aware of what is going to happen and give a few days' notice so that the idea can sink in.

Once you have outlined your strategy, work out your menus and

stick to them. Include foods your child definitely likes, chicken or carrots for instance, and obviously avoid foods your child hates although you could introduce some new foods for variety. Set yourself a time scale, perhaps one or two weeks, and review things after this period has elapsed.

PUTTING THE PLAN INTO ACTION

Begin your new plan of action when all the family are there to help, such as a weekend, and stick to it. Make a fuss of the plans so it seems more like a game than a prison sentence. Add a few flowers to the table or a pretty cloth to make it more special.

Begin the day with a normal breakfast but give the fussy eater the smallest possible portion. If the child eats it up then offer something you know your child likes, such as an apple, a few raisins or a fruit yogurt.

As the days progress, you could offer a biscuit or milkshake as a treat.

Give plenty of encouragement and praise, but be firm if the child plays up. If she behaves badly, take her to a different room or to the bottom of the stairs and explain that the only food is that on the table. Sit down with the rest of the family, leaving the fussy eater's food on the table and try to ignore the child.

If the child changes her mind just as you're about to clear away, then get the other members of the family to come back to the table and wait until the fussy eater has finished.

Continue in this way with other meals. Don't be swayed if your child says she will eat her food watching TV or if she wants her pudding first. Explain that she must eat just like everyone else or go without.

If she begins to cry, sit her down in another room and return to the table. This is perhaps the hardest thing of all.

After a few days, there should be a glimmer of progress. Still offer tiny portions of food, followed by foods that you know your child will eat as a treat. Keeping to a plan like this is hard, but if all the family sticks together and thinks positively, then it is possible. Keep to the time span you decided, then suggest you all go to your local pizza or burger restaurant and let the fussy eater choose what she likes.

Lunch Specials

Now your baby has progressed from puréed to chopped food you can begin to cook more grown-up lunches. Try to introduce a range of foods to give a balanced diet and a variety of tastes although don't be disheartened if there are a few hiccups along the way.

Sticky Chicken

Serves 2–4

4 chicken drumsticks

10ml/2 tsp oil

5ml/1 tsp soy sauce

15ml/1 tbsp smooth peanut butter

15ml/1 tbsp tomato ketchup

small jacket potatoes, sweetcorn and tomato wedges, to serve

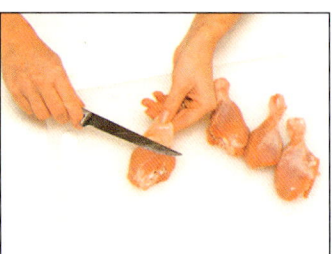

1 Preheat the oven to 200°C/400°F/Gas 6 and line a small shallow baking tin with foil. Rinse the drumsticks under cold water, pat dry and peel off the skin. Make three or four slashes in the meat with a sharp knife and place in the tin.

TIP
If more convenient, use the peanut butter and ketchup mixture over chicken thighs or kebabs instead.

2 Blend the remaining ingredients and spread thickly over the top of the chicken drumsticks. Cook in the oven for 15 minutes.

3 Turn the drumsticks over and baste with the peanut butter mixture and meat juices.

4 Cook for a further 20 minutes or until the juices run clear when the chicken is pierced with a knife.

5 Cool slightly, then wrap a small piece of foil around the base of each drumstick. Arrange on plates and serve with small jacket potatoes, hot sweetcorn and tomato wedges.

Coriander Chicken Casserole

Serves 2

2 chicken thighs
¼ small onion
1 small carrot, about 50g/2oz
1 small piece swede, about 50g/2oz
5ml/1 tsp oil
2.5ml/½ tsp ground coriander
pinch of turmeric
5ml/1 tsp plain flour
150ml/¼ pint/⅔ cup chicken stock
salt and pepper (optional)
mashed potatoes and peas, to serve

1. Preheat the oven to 180°C/350°F/Gas 4. Rinse the chicken under cold water, pat dry and trim away any excess skin if necessary. Chop the onion, carrot and swede.

2. Heat the oil in a frying pan, add the chicken and brown on each side. Add the vegetables.

TIP
Chop the meat for very young toddlers. Serve older children the whole thigh to make them feel more grown up, then help with cutting.

3. Stir in the coriander, turmeric and flour, then add the stock and a little salt and pepper, if liked. Bring to the boil then transfer to a casserole.

4. Cover and cook in the oven for 1 hour. Spoon onto serving plates or into shallow dishes, cool slightly and serve the chicken casserole with mashed potatoes and peas.

Cheesy Chicken Parcels

Serves 2

1 boned and skinned chicken breast, about 150g/5oz
25g/1oz Cheddar cheese
1 slice lean ham, cut into 4 strips
15ml/1 tbsp oil
new potatoes, broccoli and carrots, to serve

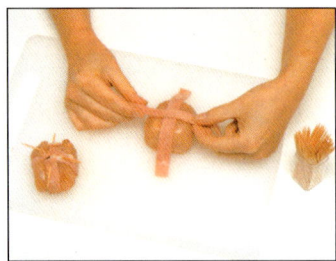

1. Rinse the chicken under cold water, pat dry and cut in half crossways. Place each half between two pieces of clear film and flatten slightly with a rolling pin until each piece is about 10cm/4in square.

2. Cut the cheese in half and place a piece on each escalope. Wrap the chicken around the cheese to enclose it completely.

3. Arrange two pieces of the ham crossways over each of the parcels, securing them underneath with cocktail sticks. Brush the chicken parcels with oil.

TIP
You could wrap the parcels with halved rashers of rindless streaky bacon, if preferred.

4. Place on a piece of foil and chill until ready to cook.

5. Preheat the grill. Cook the chicken for 10 minutes, turning once, until browned. Remove the cocktail sticks, cool slightly, then arrange on two plates and serve with new potatoes, steamed broccoli florets and sliced carrots.

Peppered Beef Casserole

Serves 2

115g/4oz lean braising steak
¼ small onion
¼ small red pepper
¼ small yellow pepper
5ml/1 tsp oil
30ml/2 tbsp canned red kidney beans, drained and rinsed
5ml/1 tsp plain flour
150ml/¼ pint/⅔ cup lamb stock
15ml/1 tbsp tomato ketchup
5ml/1 tsp Worcestershire sauce
45ml/3 tbsp couscous
a few drops of oil
40g/1½oz/3 tbsp frozen peas
salt and pepper (optional)

4 Bring to the boil, stirring, then transfer to a casserole dish, cover and cook in the oven for about 1½ hours, or until the meat is tender.

5 Just before serving place the couscous in a bowl, cover with boiling water and leave to soak for 5 minutes. Drain into a sieve and stir in a few drops of oil.

6 Bring a saucepan of water to the boil, add the peas, and place the sieve of couscous over the saucepan. Cover and cook for 5 minutes.

7 Spoon the casserole on to two plates or dishes. Fluff up the couscous with a fork, drain the peas and spoon on to the plates. Cool slightly before serving.

1 Preheat the oven to 180°C/350°F/Gas 4. Rinse the meat under cold water and pat dry. Trim away any fat and cut into small cubes. Chop the onion, remove the seeds and core from the peppers and cut into small cubes.

2 Heat the oil in a small frying pan or saucepan, add the beef and onion and fry gently until browned, stirring frequently.

3 Add the peppers and kidney beans, then stir in the flour, stock, tomato ketchup, Worcestershire sauce and a little salt and pepper if liked.

Lamb Stew

Serves 2

115g/4oz lamb fillet
¼ small onion
1 small carrot, about 50g/2oz
½ small parsnip, about 50g/2oz
1 small potato
5ml/1 tsp oil
150ml/¼ pint/⅔ cup lamb stock
pinch of dried rosemary
salt and pepper (optional)
crusty bread, to serve

1 Rinse the lamb under cold water and pat dry. Cut away any fat from the meat and cut into small cubes. Finely chop the onion, then dice the carrot and parsnip and cut the potato into slightly larger pieces.

2 Heat the oil in a medium-size saucepan, add the lamb and onion and fry gently until browned. Add the carrot, parsnip and potato and fry the lamb and vegetables for a further 3 minutes, stirring.

3 Add the lamb stock, dried rosemary and a little salt and pepper, if liked. Bring to the boil, cover and simmer for 35–40 minutes or until the meat is tender and moist.

4 Spoon the stew into shallow bowls and cool slightly before serving with crusty bread.

Mexican Mince

Serves 3–4

¼ small onion
1 strip red pepper
½ small courgette, about 50g/2oz
115g/4oz lean minced beef
1 small garlic clove, crushed
45ml/3 tbsp canned baked beans
45ml/3 tbsp beef stock
15ml/1 tbsp tomato ketchup
18 corn chips
25g/1oz/¼ cup grated Cheddar cheese
green salad, to serve

1 Finely chop the onion and dice the pepper and courgette.

2 Dry fry the onion and mince in a medium-size saucepan, stirring until browned all over.

3 Stir in the remaining ingredients and bring to the boil, stirring. Cover and simmer the mixture for 15 minutes, stirring occasionally.

4 Place the corn chips on plates, spoon on the mixture and sprinkle the grated cheese over the top. Serve with a green salad.

Lamb and Celery Casserole

Serves 2

115g/4oz lamb fillet
¼ onion
1 small carrot, about 50g/2oz
1 celery stick
25g/1oz button mushrooms
5ml/1 tsp oil
10ml/2 tsp plain flour
175ml/6fl oz/¾ cup lamb stock
bay leaf
salt and pepper (optional)
mashed potatoes and baby Brussels sprouts, to serve

1 Preheat the oven to 180°C/350°F/Gas 4. Rinse the lamb under cold water and pat dry, then trim off any fat and cut into small cubes. Chop the onion and carrot, rinse the celery and mushrooms, pat dry and slice thinly.

2 Heat the oil in a frying pan, add the lamb, onion and bay leaf and fry gently until the lamb is browned, stirring frequently. Add the remaining vegetables and fry for a further 3 minutes until they are softened and lightly brown.

VARIATION

For a more unusual flavour, substitute fennel for the celery. Its slight aniseed taste goes well with lamb.

3 Stir in the flour, then add the stock, and a little salt and pepper, if liked. Bring to the boil and then transfer to a casserole, cover and cook in the oven for 45 minutes or until the meat is tender.

4 Spoon the casserole on to plates discarding the bay leaf. Cool slightly then serve with mashed potatoes and tiny Brussels sprouts.

Shepherds' Pie

Serves 2

½ small onion
175g/6oz lean minced beef
10ml/2 tsp plain flour
30ml/2 tbsp tomato ketchup
150ml/¼ pint/⅔ cup beef stock
pinch of mixed herbs
slice swede, about 50g/2oz
½ small parsnip, about 50g/2oz
1 medium-sized potato, about 115g/4oz
10ml/2 tsp milk
15g/½oz/1 tbsp butter or margarine
½ carrot
40g/1½oz/3 tbsp frozen peas
salt and pepper (optional)

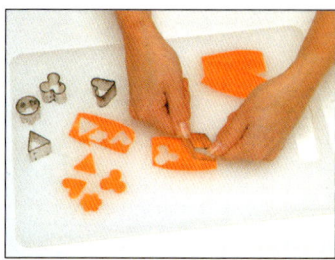

1. Preheat oven to 190°C/375°F/Gas 5. Finely chop the onion, and place in a small saucepan with the mince and dry fry over a low heat, stirring, until the mince is evenly browned.

2. Add the flour, stirring, then add the ketchup, stock, mixed herbs and seasoning, if liked. Bring to the boil, cover and simmer gently for 30 minutes, stirring occasionally.

3. Meanwhile, chop the swede, parsnip and potato and cook for 20 minutes until tender. Drain.

4. Mash with the milk and half of the butter or margarine.

5. Spoon the mince into two 250ml/8fl oz/1 cup ovenproof dishes. Place the mashed vegetables on top fluffing them up with a fork. Dot with butter or margarine.

6. Place both the pies on a baking sheet and cook for about 25–30 minutes until browned on top and bubbly.

7. Peel and thinly slice the carrot lengthways. Stamp out shapes with petits fours cutters. Cook in a saucepan of boiling water with the peas for 5 minutes. Drain and serve with the shepherds' pies. Remember that baked pies are very hot when they come out of the oven. Always allow to cool slightly before serving to children.

Tuna Fish Cakes

Serves 2–3

1 large potato, about 225g/8oz
knob of butter or margarine
10ml/2 tsp milk
5ml/1 tsp lemon juice
100g/3½oz can tuna fish
40g/1½oz/3 tbsp frozen sweetcorn, defrosted
flour, for dusting
1 egg
60ml/4 tbsp ground almonds
50g/2oz green beans
½ carrot
6 frozen peas
15ml/1 tbsp oil
salt and pepper (optional)

1 Peel and cut the potato into chunks and then cook in a saucepan of boiling water for about 15 minutes until tender.

2 Drain the potato and mash with the butter or margarine, milk, lemon juice and a little salt and pepper, if liked. Drain the tuna fish and stir into the potato with the defrosted sweetcorn.

3 Divide the mixture into six and pat each portion into a fish shape with floured hands.

4 Beat the egg in a dish and place the ground almonds on a plate. Dip the fish cakes into the egg and then into the almonds making sure they are completely covered. Place on a floured plate and chill until ready to cook.

5 Trim the beans, peel and cut the carrot into sticks a little smaller than the beans. Cook in a pan of boiling water with the peas for about 5 minutes.

6 Meanwhile heat the oil in a frying pan, and fry the fish cakes for 5 minutes until golden brown and crisp, turning once.

7 Drain and arrange on serving plates with pea "eyes" and bean and carrot "pond weed". Cool slightly before serving.

Cheesy Fish Pies

Serves 2

1 medium-sized potato, about 150g/5oz
25g/1oz green cabbage
115g/4oz cod or hoki fillets
25g/1oz/2 tbsp frozen sweetcorn
150ml/¼ pint/⅔ cup milk
15ml/1 tbsp butter or margarine
15ml/1 tbsp plain flour
25g/1oz/¼ cup grated red Leicester cheese
5ml/1 tsp sesame seeds
carrots and mange tout, to serve

1. Peel and cut the potato into chunks and shred the cabbage. Cut any skin away from the fish fillets and rinse under cold water.

2. Bring a saucepan of water to the boil, add the potato and cook for 10 minutes. Add the cabbage and cook for a further 5 minutes until tender. Drain.

3. Meanwhile place the fish fillets, the sweetcorn and all but 10ml/2 tsp of the milk in a second saucepan. Bring to the boil then cover the saucepan and simmer very gently for 8–10 minutes until the fish flakes easily when pressed with a knife.

4. Strain the fish and sweetcorn, reserving the cooking liquid. Wash the pan then melt the butter or margarine in the pan. Stir in the flour then gradually add the reserved cooking liquid and bring to the boil, stirring until thickened and smooth.

5. Add the fish and sweetcorn with half of the grated cheese. Spoon into two small ovenproof dishes.

6. Mash the potato and cabbage with the remaining 10ml/2 tsp milk. Stir in half of the remaining cheese and spoon the mixture over the fish. Sprinkle with the sesame seeds and the remaining cheese.

7. Cook under a preheated grill until the topping is browned. Cool slightly before serving with vegetable fishes.

Surprise Haddock Parcels

Serves 2

| ½ small courgette, about 50g/2oz |
| 175g/6oz smoked haddock |
| 1 small tomato |
| knob of butter or margarine |
| pinch of dried mixed herbs |
| new potatoes and broccoli, to serve |

1. Preheat the oven to 200°C/400°F/Gas 6. Tear off two pieces of foil, then trim and thinly slice the courgette and divide equally between the two pieces of foil.

2. Cut the skin away from the fish, remove any bones, cut into two equal pieces and rinse under cold water. Pat the haddock dry and place on top of the courgettes.

3. Slice the tomato and arrange slices on top of each piece of haddock. Add a little butter or margarine to each and sprinkle with mixed herbs.

4. Wrap the foil around the fish and seal the edges of each to make two parcels, then place the parcels on a baking sheet and cook in the oven for 15–20 minutes depending on the thickness of the fish.

5. To test for doneness, open up one of the parcels and insert a knife into the centre. If the fish flakes easily then it is ready.

6. Cool slightly then arrange the parcels on plates and serve with new potatoes and broccoli.

Cowboy Bangers and Beans

Serves 2

3 chipolata sausages
¼ small onion
1 small carrot, about 50g/2oz
1 strip red pepper
5ml/1 tsp oil
200g/7oz can baked beans
10ml/2 tsp Worcestershire sauce
fingers of toast, to serve

1 Press the centre of each sausage, twist and cut in half to make two small sausages.

2 Finely chop the onion, then dice the carrot and the pepper, discarding the core and seeds.

3 Heat the oil in a frying pan, add the sausages and the chopped onion and fry until browned.

TIP
Check the beans towards the end of cooking, you may need to add a little extra water.

4 Add the remaining ingredients and stir in 30ml/2 tbsp water. Cover and cook for 15 minutes or until the carrot is cooked.

5 Spoon on to serving plates or into dishes, cool slightly and serve with fingers of toast.

Mini Toad-in-the-Hole

Serves 2

3 chipolata sausages
5ml/1 tsp oil
60ml/4 tbsp plain flour
1 egg
60ml/4 tbsp milk
salt
baked beans and green beans, to serve

1 Preheat the oven to 220°C/425°F/Gas 7. Press the centre of each sausage with your finger, twist and then cut in half. Brush two 10cm/4in Yorkshire pudding tins with oil. Add the sausages and cook for about 5 minutes.

2 Place the flour, egg and a pinch of salt in a bowl. Gradually whisk in the milk, beating until a smooth batter is formed.

3 Pour into the tins, quickly return to the oven and bake for 15 minutes until risen and golden.

4 Loosen with a knife and turn out on to serving plates. Cool slightly and serve with baked beans and steamed green beans.

Pork Hot-pot

Serves 2

175g/6oz lean pork
¼ small onion
5ml/1 tsp oil
5ml/1 tsp plain flour
150ml/¼ pint/⅔ cup chicken stock
40g/1½oz/3 tbsp frozen sweetcorn
pinch of dried sage
1 medium potato, about 150g/5oz
1 carrot, about 75g/3oz
knob of butter or margarine
salt and pepper (optional)
broccoli and Brussels sprouts, to serve

1 Preheat the oven to 180°C/350°F/Gas 4. Rinse the pork under cold water, pat dry, trim away any fat and cut into small cubes. Peel and finely chop the onion.

2 Heat the oil in a frying pan, add the cubed pork and onion and fry until golden brown, stirring.

3 Add in the flour and stir until blended, then add the sweetcorn, dried sage, stock and a little salt and pepper, if liked. Bring to the boil and then turn the mixture into a shallow ovenproof dish.

4 Peel and thinly slice the potato and carrot. Arrange slices so that they overlap on top of the pork mixture. Dot with butter or margarine. Cover with foil and cook in the oven for about 1 hour until the potatoes are tender.

5 Remove the foil and brown under the grill if liked. Spoon on to serving plates, cool slightly, then serve with steamed broccoli and tiny Brussels sprouts.

TIP
If you only have one child, make the hot-pots in two dishes. Cool one, cover with clear film and freeze for up to three months.

Pork and Lentil Casserole

Serves 2

175g/6oz boneless spare rib pork chop
¼ small onion
1 small carrot, about 50g/2oz
5ml/1 tsp oil
1 small garlic clove, crushed
25g/1oz red lentils
90ml/6 tbsp canned chopped tomatoes
90ml/6 tbsp chicken stock
salt and pepper (optional)
swede and peas, to serve

1 Preheat the oven to 180°C/350°F/Gas 4. Trim off any excess fat from the pork and cut in half. Finely chop the onion and dice the carrot.

2 Heat the oil in a frying pan, add the pork and onion and fry until the pork is browned on both sides.

3 Add the garlic, lentils and carrots and stir gently to mix.

4 Pour in the chopped tomatoes, stock and seasoning, if liked, and cook briefly to bring to the boil. Transfer to a casserole, cover and cook in the oven for 1¼ hours.

5 Spoon portions on to serving plates or shallow dishes and cool slightly. Serve with diced buttered swede and peas.

TIP
Teaching a child to use a knife and fork can be frustrating. Spare rib pork chops are wonderfully tender when casseroled and so very easy to cut with a child's knife.

Sticky Ribs and Apple Slaw

Serves 2

225g/8oz short pork ribs
10ml/2 tsp oil
10ml/2 tsp tomato ketchup
10ml/2 tsp Hoi sin sauce
1 medium potato, scrubbed but not peeled
knob of butter or margarine

For the Apple Slaw

½ carrot
½ eating apple
25g/1oz white cabbage
10ml/2 tsp sultanas
30ml/2 tbsp mayonnaise
carrot slices, tomato wedges and celery sticks, to serve

4 Meanwhile peel the carrot and peel, quarter and core the apple. Coarsely grate the apple and carrot and finely chop the cabbage.

5 Place in a bowl with the sultanas and mayonnaise and mix well.

6 Arrange the ribs on serving plates. Halve the baked potato and add a little butter or margarine to each half and serve with the pork ribs together with star-shaped carrot slices, celery sticks and tomato wedges and spoonfuls of coleslaw.

TIP
Check the temperature of the ribs before serving as they stay very hot for a surprisingly long time. Nothing will put a child off more than food that is very hot. Toddlers prefer their food to be lukewarm.

1 Preheat the oven to 200°C/400°F/Gas 6. Rinse the pork ribs under cold water, pat dry and put on a roasting rack set over a small roasting tin. Mix the oil, ketchup and Hoi sin sauce and brush over the ribs, reserving any extra mixture.

2 Pour a little boiling water into the base of the roasting tin. Prick the potato all over with a fork and then place in the oven with the spare ribs, preferably on the same shelf.

3 Cook for 1 hour, turning the pork ribs once during cooking and brushing with any of the remaining ketchup mixture.

Mini Cheese and Ham Tarts

Makes 12

For the Pastry

115g/4oz/1 cup plain flour

50g/2oz/4 tbsp sunflower margarine

For the Filling

50g/2oz/½ cup Cheddar cheese

2 slices wafer thin ham, chopped

75g/3oz/½ cup frozen sweetcorn

1 egg

120ml/4fl oz/½ cup milk

pinch of paprika

salt and pepper

carrot and cucumber sticks, to serve

1 Preheat the oven to 200°C/400°F/Gas 6. Place the flour in a bowl, add the margarine and rub in with fingertips until the mixture resembles fine breadcrumbs.

2 Stir in 20ml/4 tsp water and mix to make a smooth dough. Lightly knead and roll out thinly on a floured surface.

3 Stamp out twelve 7.5cm/3in circles with a fluted biscuit cutter, rerolling the pastry as necessary. Press into a bun tray.

TIP
Encourage children to eat more vegetables by serving them with a yogurt dip flavoured with tomato purée.

4 Grate the cheese, mix with the ham and sweetcorn and divide among the pastry cases.

5 Beat together the egg, milk, salt and pepper and pour into the tarts. Sprinkle with paprika.

6 Cook in the oven for 12–15 minutes until well risen and browned. Serve warm with carrot and cucumber sticks.

Going Green

Getting children to eat more than a few frozen peas and the odd carrot can be an uphill battle. Encourage them to be a little more adventurous by mixing their favourite foods with some new vegetables.

Pick-up Sticks

Serves 2

5cm/2in piece of leek
25g/1oz green beans
1 strip red pepper
1 celery stick
25g/1oz bean sprouts
1 small carrot, about 50g/2oz
5ml/1 tsp oil
15ml/1 tbsp tomato ketchup
5ml/1 tsp soy sauce
pinch ground ginger
grilled sausages, to serve

1 Rinse the leek, beans, pepper, celery and bean sprouts. Peel the carrot. Halve any large beans and bean sprouts. Cut the remaining vegetables into thin strips.

2 Heat the oil in a frying pan, add all the vegetables except the bean sprouts and fry for 3 minutes, stirring all the time.

3 Add the bean sprouts, ketchup, soy sauce, ginger and 10ml/2 tsp water. Cook for a further 2 minutes, stirring until the vegetables are hot.

4 Spoon on to serving plates and leave to cool slightly. Serve with grilled sausages.

TIP
Don't overcook the vegetables. They should be quite crisp, and firm enough for your child to pick up.

Saucy Spinach Pancakes

Serves 2–3

50g/2oz fresh spinach, leaves only
50g/2oz plain flour
1 egg yolk
300ml/½ pint/1¼ cups milk
15ml/1 tbsp margarine
15ml/1 tbsp plain flour
25g/1oz/¼ cup grated red Leicester cheese
40g/1½oz wafer thin ham, chopped
40g/1½oz button mushrooms, thinly sliced
15ml/1 tbsp oil

1 Wash the spinach leaves well in cold water and then place in a frying pan, set over a medium heat. Cover and cook gently for 2–3 minutes until the spinach has just wilted, stirring occasionally. Drain off any excess liquid and cool.

2 Put the flour, egg yolk and a little salt and pepper, if liked, into a bowl. Whisk in half of the milk to make a smooth batter. Finely chop the spinach and stir into the batter.

3 Melt the margarine in a saucepan, stir in the flour and then gradually stir in the remaining milk and bring to the boil, stirring continuously until smooth. Add the cheese, ham and mushrooms and stir to mix. Heat, cover and keep warm.

4 Heat a little oil in a frying pan, pour off excess then add 30ml/ 2 tbsp pancake batter, tilting the pan so that the batter covers the base. Cook for a few minutes until browned, then flip over and cook the other side until golden. Slide the pancake on to a plate and keep warm.

5 Continue making pancakes until all the batter is used up.

6 Fold the pancakes into quarters then spoon a little of the ham mixture into each one. Arrange the pancakes on plates and serve with tomato wedges and new potatoes.

TIP
If offering spinach to your child for the first time make sure that the filling includes foods that you know are liked. Omit or add ingredients as necessary.

Broccoli and Cauliflower Cheese

Serves 2

1 egg
75g/3oz broccoli
75g/3oz cauliflower
15g/½oz/1 tbsp margarine
15ml/1 tbsp plain flour
150ml/¼ pint/⅔ cup milk
40g/1½oz/⅓ cup grated red Leicester cheese
½ tomato
salt and pepper (optional)

1. Put the egg in a small saucepan of cold water, bring to the boil and cook for about 10 minutes until the egg is hard-boiled.

2. Meanwhile cut the broccoli and cauliflower into florets and thinly slice the broccoli stalks. Cook in a saucepan of boiling water for about 8 minutes until just tender.

3. Drain the vegetables and dry the pan. Melt the margarine, stir in the flour then gradually mix in the milk and bring to the boil, stirring until thickened and smooth.

4. Stir two-thirds of the cheese into the sauce together with a little seasoning, if liked. Reserve two of the broccoli florets and stir the remaining vegetables into the sauce.

5. Divide the mixture between two heat-resistant shallow dishes and sprinkle with the remaining cheese.

6. Place under a hot grill until golden brown and bubbling.

7. Make a face on each dish with broccoli florets for a nose, a halved tomato for a mouth and peeled and sliced hard-boiled egg for eyes. Cool slightly before serving.

TIP

Making a face or fun pattern can be just enough to tempt a fussy eater to try something new.

Potato Boats

Serves 2

2 small baking potatoes
5cm/2in piece leek
25g/1oz button mushrooms
10ml/2 tsp oil
25g/1oz/2 tbsp frozen sweetcorn
15ml/1 tbsp milk
knob of butter
½ courgette, about 50g/2oz, grated
1 carrot, about 50g/2oz, grated
2 slices processed cheese
1 slice ham
salt and pepper (optional)

1. Preheat the oven to 200°C/400°F/Gas 6. Prick the potatoes with a fork and bake for 1 hour until soft. Alternatively, prick well and then microwave on a sheet of kitchen paper on High (full power) for 7–8 minutes.

2. Halve the leek lengthways, wash thoroughly to remove any grit and then slice thinly. Rinse the mushrooms, pat dry and thinly slice.

3. Heat 5ml/1 tsp oil in a frying pan and gently fry the leek, mushrooms and sweetcorn for about 3 minutes until softened, stirring frequently. Turn into a bowl and keep warm.

4. When the potatoes are cooked, cut in half and scoop the centres into the bowl with the leek and mushroom mixture. Add the milk, butter and a little salt and pepper if liked, and stir to mix. Pile the mixture back into the potato shells.

5. Reheat the remaining 5ml/1 tsp of oil and fry the grated courgette and carrot for 2 minutes until softened. Spoon on to two small plates and spread with a fork to cover the bases of the plates.

6. Arrange two potato halves on each plate. For sails, cut the cheese and ham into triangles and secure to potatoes with cocktail sticks. Cool slightly before serving.

Fat Cats

Serves 2

oil, for greasing
200g/7oz frozen puff pastry, defrosted
a little flour, for dusting
beaten egg, to glaze
50g/2oz broccoli
25g/1oz/2 tbsp frozen mixed vegetables
15ml/1 tbsp butter or margarine
15ml/1 tbsp plain flour
100ml/3½fl oz/½ cup milk
30ml/2 tbsp grated Cheddar cheese
a little mustard and cress, to garnish

1 Preheat the oven to 220°C/425°F/Gas 7 and lightly brush a baking sheet with a little oil. Roll out the pastry thinly on a surface lightly dusted with a little flour.

2 Using a shaped biscuit cutter, stamp out four 13cm/5in cat shapes. Place two cats on the baking sheet and brush with egg.

3 Cut a large hole in the centre of the two remaining cats and gently place the shapes on top of the other two cats.

VARIATION
Ring the changes by making this recipe using different shaped biscuit cutters to cut out the pastry shapes. Get your child to choose his favourite.

4 Brush the tops with egg and cook for 10 minutes until the pastry is well risen and golden.

5 Meanwhile chop the broccoli and cook in a small saucepan of boiling water with the frozen vegetables for 5 minutes. Drain.

6 Dry the pan and melt the butter or margarine. Stir in the flour and then gradually add the milk. Bring to the boil, stirring all the time until thickened and smooth.

7 Reserve two peas and two pieces of carrot for garnish and then stir the remaining vegetables into the sauce with the grated cheese.

8 Enlarge the cavity in the centre of each pastry cat by scooping out a little of the pastry. Spoon in the vegetable mixture and arrange on two serving plates. Garnish with halved peas for eyes, halved carrot strips for whiskers and red pepper noses. Add mustard and cress grass. Cool slightly before serving.

Potato, Carrot and Courgette Rösti

Serves 2–4

1 small potato, about 115g/4oz
½ carrot, about 25g/1oz
½ courgette, about 25g/1oz
10ml/2 tsp sunflower oil
sausages and baked beans, to serve

1. Grate the potato, carrot and courgette into a bowl and mix together thoroughly.

2. Place several sheets of kitchen paper on a surface and put the vegetables on top. Cover with more kitchen paper and press down to soak up all the excess liquid.

3. Heat the oil in a frying pan and spoon the vegetables into the pan to form eight rounds. Flatten slightly with a fork and fry four of the rounds for 5 minutes, turning once until the potatoes are thoroughly cooked and the rösti is golden brown on both sides.

4. Lift out of the pan and cook the remaining mixture. Cool slightly and serve with grilled sausages and baked beans.

Veggie Burgers

Serves 2–4

1 large or 2 small potatoes, about 225g/8oz
1 carrot, about 50g/2oz
25g/1oz broccoli
25g/1oz Brussels sprouts
1 egg yolk
15ml/1 tbsp plain flour
15ml/1 tbsp freshly grated Parmesan cheese
15ml/1 tbsp oil
salt and pepper (optional)
canned spaghetti hoops, pieces of cucumber, strips of ham and tomato ketchup, to serve

1. Cut the potato and carrot into chunks and cook in boiling water for 15 minutes until tender.

2. Meanwhile, cut the broccoli into small florets, chop the stem finely and thinly slice the Brussels sprouts. Rinse under cold water then add to the potatoes and carrots for the last 5 minutes of cooking.

3. Drain the vegetables thoroughly and then mash together. Add the egg yolk and a little salt and pepper, if liked, then mix well.

4. Divide into four and shape into burgers with floured hands. Coat in flour and Parmesan cheese.

5. Heat the oil in a frying pan, add the burgers and fry for 5 minutes, turning once until golden brown. Cool slightly then serve with canned spaghetti hoops, strips of ham, a few cucumber wedges and a little tomato ketchup. Add a face with peas, carrot and cucumber.

TIP
To make a spider add cooked green bean legs, a red pepper mouth and yellow pepper eyes.

Vegetable Lasagne

Serves 2–3

¼ small onion
50g/2oz carrot
50g/2oz courgette
50g/2oz aubergine
25g/1oz button mushrooms
10ml/2 tsp oil
1 small garlic clove, crushed
225g/8oz can chopped tomatoes
pinch of mixed herbs
15ml/1 tbsp butter or margarine
15ml/1 tbsp plain flour
150ml/¼ pint/⅔ cup milk
60ml/4 tbsp grated cheese
3 sheets pre-cooked lasagne
salt and pepper
mixed salad, to serve

1 Finely chop the onion and carrot, and finely dice the courgette and aubergine. Wipe and thinly slice the mushrooms.

2 Heat the oil and fry the vegetables for 3 minutes until softened. Add the garlic, tomatoes and herbs, then bring to the boil, cover and simmer for 5 minutes.

3 Melt the butter or margarine in a saucepan, stir in the flour. Add the milk and bring to the boil, stirring, until thickened. Stir in half of the grated cheese and a little salt and pepper.

4 Preheat the oven to 180°C/350°F/Gas 4. Spoon one-third of the vegetable mixture into the base of an ovenproof dish, then add a little sauce. Add a slice of lasagne then cover with half of the remaining vegetable mixture and half the remaining sauce.

5 Add a second sheet of pasta and top with the remaining vegetable mixture. Add a third sheet of lasagne and top with the remaining cheese sauce. Sprinkle with the remaining cheese.

6 Cook for 50–60 minutes, checking after 30 minutes and covering loosely with foil if the topping is browning too quickly. Spoon on to serving plates and leave the lasagne to cool slightly. Serve with a little mixed salad.

Aubergine Bolognese

Serves 2

50g/2oz aubergine
1 strip red pepper
1 strip yellow pepper
5cm/2in piece of leek
1 carrot, about 50g/2oz
10ml/2 tsp oil
1 small garlic clove, crushed
25g/1oz/2 tbsp frozen sweetcorn
25g/1oz/2 tbsp red lentils
225g/8oz can chopped tomatoes
250ml/8fl oz/1 cup vegetable stock
pinch of dried herbs
50g/2oz dried pasta shapes
knob of butter or margarine
30ml/2 tbsp grated cheese (optional)
salt and pepper

1 Rinse the aubergine, peppers and leek, peel the carrot and then finely dice all the vegetables.

2 Heat the oil in a medium-sized saucepan, add the diced vegetables and gently fry for 3 minutes, stirring frequently, until they are slightly softened.

TIP
Sprinkle the diced aubergine with salt, leave to drain in a colander for 30 minutes, then rinse. This removes any bitter taste.

3 Add the garlic, sweetcorn, lentils, tomatoes, stock, herbs and a little salt and pepper.

4 Bring to the boil, cover and simmer for about 30 minutes, stirring occasionally and adding a little extra stock if necessary.

5 In the last 10 minutes of cooking, bring a pan of water to the boil and add the pasta. Cook for 10 minutes until tender.

6 Drain, toss in a little butter or margarine. Spoon on to plates and top with the aubergine bolognese. Sprinkle with cheese.

Quick Teas

If you've had a day rushing around, then rustle up these quick and tasty toddlers' teas – they all cook in 10 minutes or less. There is a wide variety of recipes to choose from. Remember the importance of fun presentation, to tempt your toddler to try new foods.

Speedy Chicken Pie

Serves 2

| 1 celery stick |
| 25g/1oz/2 tbsp frozen sweetcorn, defrosted |
| 30ml/2 tbsp mayonnaise |
| 2.5ml/½ tsp ground coriander |
| 75g/3oz cold cooked chicken |
| ½ small packet plain crisps |
| 15ml/1 tbsp grated red Leicester cheese |
| salt and pepper (optional) |
| peas and broccoli, to serve |

2 Spoon into a shallow ovenproof dish and level the surface.

3 Roughly crush the crisps and sprinkle over the chicken. Top with the grated cheese and cook for 10 minutes until hot and bubbly.

4 Cool slightly then serve the pie with peas and broccoli.

1 Preheat the oven to 220°C/425°F/Gas 7. Rinse the celery, slice thinly and place in a bowl with the sweetcorn, mayonnaise, ground coriander and a little salt and pepper, if liked. Dice the chicken, add to the bowl and mix well.

Variation
Mexican Chicken Pie
Replace the ground coriander with ground cumin and replace the crisps with about 30ml/2 tbsp crumbled plain tortilla chips.

Skinny Dippers

Serves 2

150g/5oz boneless, skinless chicken breast
25g/1oz/¼ cup grated Cheddar cheese
50g/2oz/1 cup fresh breadcrumbs
15g/½oz/1 tbsp butter or margarine
115g/4oz frozen oven chips
½ small carrot, cut into thin strips
½ small courgette, cut into thin strips
45ml/3 tbsp tomato ketchup

1 Rinse the chicken under cold water and pat dry with kitchen paper. Cut into thin strips.

2 Mix the grated cheese and breadcrumbs on a plate. Melt the butter or margarine in a small saucepan or in a dish in the microwave on High (full power) for 20 seconds, then toss the chicken strips in the butter or margarine and roll in the breadcrumb mixture.

3 Arrange the chicken and chips on a foiled-lined baking sheet. Preheat the grill and bring a saucepan of water to the boil.

4 Grill the chicken for 6–8 minutes and the chips 8–10 minutes until both are well browned, turning once. When the chicken is ready, keep warm in a shallow dish while the chips finish cooking.

5 Cook the vegetables for 5 minutes in the pan of boiling water until tender.

6 Spoon the ketchup into two ramekins or egg cups and place in the centre of two serving plates. Drain the vegetables and divide the vegetables, chicken and chips between the two plates. Allow to cool slightly before dipping into ketchup.

TIP
Keep a supply of fresh breadcrumbs in a sealed plastic bag in the freezer. There is no need to defrost, just take out as much as you need and use from frozen.

Sweet and Sour Chicken

Serves 2

50g/2oz/¼ cup long grain white rice
1 carrot, about 50g/2oz
1 courgette, about 50g/2oz
2 skinless chicken thighs
10ml/2 tsp oil
25g/1oz/2 tbsp frozen peas
5ml/1 tsp cornflour
5ml/1 tsp soy sauce
10ml/2 tsp tomato ketchup
60ml/4 tbsp orange juice
1 egg, beaten

1 Cook the rice in boiling water for 8–10 minutes until tender.

2 Meanwhile, peel the carrot, trim the courgette and cut both into thin strips. Bone the chicken and cut into small chunks.

3 Heat 5ml/1 tsp of the oil in a frying pan, add the carrot, courgette, chicken and peas and fry for 5 minutes, stirring occasionally.

4 Blend the cornflour with the soy sauce and then stir into the pan together with the ketchup and orange juice. Cook gently, stirring all the time, until the sauce is glossy and has thickened.

TIP
Make the meal into an occasion and serve the food in Chinese bowls with Chinese spoons – chopsticks may be a little too tricky to manage. All children love the idea of eating in a restaurant with a parent to wait on them.

5 Drain the rice thoroughly. Add the remaining oil to the rice together with the beaten egg and cook over a gentle heat stirring until the egg has scrambled.

6 Spoon the rice and sweet and sour chicken on to serving plates and cool slightly before serving.

Ham and Tomato Scramble

Serves 2

2 slices ham
1 tomato
1 small strip yellow pepper
2 eggs
15ml/1 tbsp milk
2 slices bread
a little butter
salt

1. Finely chop the ham. Halve the tomato, scoop out and discard the seeds then chop into small dice. Finely chop the strip of pepper.

2. Beat the eggs and milk together and season with a little salt. Toast the bread lightly.

3. Heat a small knob of butter in a saucepan, add the eggs, ham, tomato and pepper and cook gently, stirring all the time until cooked to taste. Cool slightly.

4. Butter the toast and cut into shapes with small fancy-shaped biscuit cutters. Arrange on plates with the ham and tomato scramble.

TIP
If you don't have any special cutters then cut the toast into tiny triangles and squares with a knife.

Ham Salad Clown

Serves 2

2 slices ham
1 cherry tomato
2 slices apple
1 slice cheese
2 currants
2 slices hard-boiled egg
a little mustard and cress
2 long slices carrot

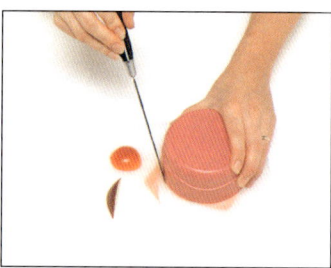

1. Cut two large rounds from the slices of ham using a biscuit cutter or the top of a glass or other container as a guide. Arrange on two plates and add a halved tomato for a nose and slice of apple for a mouth, trimming if needed.

2. Cut out small triangles or stars of cheese with a knife for eyes, place on the ham and add halved currants for eye balls.

3. Halve the egg slices and add to the face for ears. Snip the mustard and cress for hair and use snipped pieces of carrot for a ruff.

TIP
Have fun varying the ingredients for the clown. Use cheese slices, radishes, peaches, raisins, lettuce and red pepper to change the appearance and features.

Spanish Omelette

Serves 2

2 slices wafer thin ham
1 strip red pepper
15ml/1 tbsp frozen peas
50g/2oz frozen oven chips
5ml/1 tsp oil
1 egg
salt and pepper (optional)
tomato wedges, to serve

1. Chop the ham and pepper. Mix the pepper and peas. Slice the oven chips.

2. Heat the oil in a non-stick frying pan, and fry the chips for 5 minutes, stirring, until lightly browned. Add the pepper and peas and cook, stirring, for a further 2 minutes. Stir in the chopped ham.

3. Beat together the egg, 10ml/ 2 tsp water and a little salt and pepper, if liked, and pour into the pan, tilting it so that the egg mixture covers the base evenly.

4. Cook over a medium-low heat for 2–3 minutes until the base of the omelette is set and browned. Loosen the edges and invert the pan on to a plate to turn out the omelette. Then slide the omelette back into the pan and cook the second side for a few more minutes until golden.

5. Cut the omelette into wedges, arrange on two plates and cool slightly. Serve with tomato wedges.

Saucy Ham Pasta

Serves 2

50g/2oz dried pasta shapes

50g/2oz/½ cup frozen mixed vegetables

30ml/2 tbsp margarine

30ml/2 tbsp plain flour

150ml/¼ pint/⅔ cup milk

50g/2oz/½ cup grated red Leicester or Cheddar cheese

2 slices ham, chopped

salt and pepper

1 Cook the pasta in a saucepan of boiling water for 5 minutes. Add vegetables and cook for 5 more minutes until pasta is tender. Drain.

2 Melt the margarine in a medium-sized pan and stir in the flour. Gradually add the milk and bring to the boil, stirring, until the sauce is thickened and smooth.

3 Stir two-thirds of the grated cheese into the sauce and add the drained pasta and vegetables, the ham and a little salt and pepper.

4 Spoon into two shallow dishes and sprinkle with the remaining cheese. Cool slightly if necessary.

TIP
This recipe also works well if you use a 100g/3½oz can tuna, drained, in place of the ham. You could serve the ham and vegetable sauce with rice, if you prefer.

Quickie Kebabs

Serves 2–3

1 tomato
3 slices ham
½ small yellow pepper
6 button mushrooms
6 cocktail sausages
10ml/2 tsp tomato ketchup
10ml/2 tsp oil
canned spaghetti, to serve

1 Preheat the grill. Cut the tomato into six wedges and cut each slice of ham into two strips. Roll up each strip. Cut the pepper into six chunks, discarding any seeds. Wipe the mushrooms.

2 Make six kebabs by threading a tomato wedge, a ham roll, a piece of pepper, a mushroom, and a sausage on to six cocktail sticks.

TIP
Use two rashers of rindless bacon, if preferred. Halve and roll up and use in place of the ham.

3 Line a grill pan with foil and arrange the kebabs on top. Blend the ketchup and oil and brush over the kebabs. Grill for 10 minutes, turning once and brushing with the juices until the vegetables are browned and the sausages are thoroughly cooked.

4 Cool slightly then arrange on plates with canned spaghetti.

Sausage Wrappers

Serves 2

4 slices ham
10ml/2 tsp tomato relish or barbecue sauce
4 sausages
baked beans and grilled potato shapes, to serve

1 Spread one side of each slice of ham with relish or sauce.

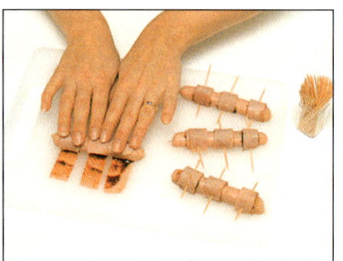

2 Cut each piece of ham into three thin strips and then wrap each sausage in three strips securing them in place with cocktail sticks.

3 Grill for 10 minutes, turning several times until the ham is browned and crisp.

4 Cool slightly then remove the cocktail sticks and serve the sausage wrappers with baked beans and grilled potato shapes.

TIP
Use four pieces of rindless streaky bacon instead of ham, if preferred.

Corned Beef Hash

Serves 2

1 potato, about 175g/6oz
10ml/2 tsp oil
50g/2oz green cabbage
115g/4oz corned beef
pinch of turmeric
15ml/1 tbsp tomato ketchup
hard-boiled egg slices, to garnish

1 Dice the potato and cook in a saucepan of boiling water for 3–4 minutes until softened. Drain.

2 Heat the oil in a medium-sized frying pan, add the diced potato and fry for 3 minutes until golden.

3 Meanwhile, chop the cabbage and dice the corned beef.

4 Add the cabbage and turmeric to the pan with the potatoes and cook for 2 minutes. Stir in the corned beef and cook for 2 minutes.

5 Stir in the ketchup and spoon on to two plates. Cool slightly before serving. Garnish with the hard-boiled egg slices.

TIP
The hash can be garnished with tomato wedges, if liked.

Cannibal Necklaces

Serves 2

45ml/3 tbsp stuffing mix
60ml/4 tbsp boiling water
115g/4oz lean minced beef
5ml/1 tsp oil
½ carrot
1 strip red pepper
1 strip green pepper
a little tomato ketchup

1 Put the stuffing mix in a bowl and pour over the boiling water. Set aside for 5 minutes to soak.

2 Stir the mince into the stuffing mix and shape into 10 small balls with floured hands.

3 Preheat the grill. Arrange the meat balls on a piece of foil on top of the grill pan and brush lightly with a little oil. Grill for 7–8 minutes, until well browned, turning once during cooking.

4 Meanwhile thinly slice the carrot and cut the pepper into chunks, discarding the core and seeds.

5 Arrange the meat balls around the bottom edge of two serving plates. Leave spaces in between.

TIP
If you're feeling adventurous, liven up simple teas by piping the child's initials on to the edge of the plate, the appropriate number for their age or even a short word like "hello".

6 Place carrot and pieces of red and green pepper between each meat ball and complete with a line and bow of ketchup for necklace strings, straight from the bottle, or pipe the ketchup if preferred.

Beef and Mushroom Burgers

Serves 2

¼ small onion
25g/1oz button mushrooms
115g/4oz lean minced beef
115g/4oz frozen oven chips
2 burger buns
10ml/2 tsp tomato ketchup
1 tomato
salt and pepper (optional)

1 Finely chop the onion, wipe and chop the mushrooms. Place the mince in a mixing bowl, add the onion and mushrooms and a little salt and pepper, if liked, and mix together thoroughly. Alternatively blend the mixture in a processor.

2 With floured hands shape two 7.5cm/3in burgers or press the mixture into a plastic burger press or upturned pastry cutter.

3 Preheat the grill. Tear off two large pieces of foil. Fold up the edges and place on a grill pan. Put the burgers on one piece and the chips on the other.

4 Cook the burgers and chips for 10 minutes turning the food once. Remove from the grill rack and keep warm. Split the burger buns in half and toast on one side only.

5 Spread the bases of the buns with ketchup, slice the tomato and place on the buns. Top each with a burger and the second bun half. Cut in half and arrange on serving plates with the chips. Cool slightly if necessary before serving.

Four Fast Fishes

Serves 2

115g/4oz hoki or cod fillet
½ egg, beaten
60ml/4 tbsp fresh breadcrumbs
10ml/2 tsp sesame seeds
10ml/2 tsp oil
15ml/1 tbsp frozen peas
4 frozen sweetcorn niblets
1 carrot
canned spaghetti rings, to serve

1 Cut away and discard any skin from the fish and rinse. Pat dry and cut into four pieces.

2 Put the egg in a saucer and place the breadcrumbs and sesame seeds on a plate. Dip pieces of fish in egg and then in breadcrumb mixture to coat the fish.

3 Heat the oil in a frying pan, add the fish and fry for 4–5 minutes, turning once, until the fish pieces are golden brown and cooked.

4 Meanwhile cook the peas and sweetcorn in a saucepan of boiling water for 5 minutes. Cut the carrot into long thin slices and then cut out fin and tail shapes and tiny triangles for mouths.

5 Arrange the pieces of fish on two plates with the carrot decorations, sweetcorn for eyes and peas for bubbles. Serve with warmed canned spaghetti rings.

TIP
You can freeze the uncooked breaded portions to provide a quick meal at a later date when you are pushed for time. Freeze them on a tray and then wrap them well to prevent the odour tainting other food in the freezer.

Tuna Risotto

Serves 2

5ml/1 tsp oil
¼ onion, finely chopped
50g/2oz long grain white rice
50g/2oz frozen mixed vegetables
1 small garlic clove, crushed
10ml/2 tsp tomato ketchup
100g/3½oz can tuna fish in water
salt and pepper (optional)

1 Heat the oil in a small saucepan and fry the chopped onion for about 3 minutes until softened.

2 Add the rice, mixed vegetables, garlic, tomato ketchup and 250ml/8fl oz/1 cup water and a little salt and pepper, if liked.

TIP
If liked use cold leftover cooked chicken, lamb or beef in place of the tuna.

3 Bring to the boil and simmer uncovered for 10 minutes. Drain the tuna and add to the rice mixture, stirring to mix. Cook for 3–4 minutes, stirring occasionally, until the water has been absorbed by the rice and the rice is tender.

4 Spoon on to plates and cool slightly before serving.

Fish Finger Log Cabins

Serves 2

4 frozen fishfingers
25g/1oz green cabbage
8 mange-tout
2 frozen peas
1 strip green pepper
1 strip red pepper

1 Grill the fishfingers for 10 minutes, turning once until golden. Meanwhile finely shred the cabbage and cook in boiling water for 3 minutes. Add the mange-tout and peas and cook for a further 2 minutes. Drain well.

2 Arrange two fishfingers side by side on each plate. Trim the mange-tout and use them to make a roof, slightly overlapping the edges of the fishfingers.

VARIATION
Sausage Log Cabin
Use four grilled cocktail chipolata sausages for each cabin. Make the roof from green beans and use shredded spinach for the grass.

3 Cut four windows from the green pepper and two doors from the red pepper and add to the log cabins, using peas as door handles. Arrange the shredded cabbage to look like grass.

Toast Toppers

All children, even the fussiest of diners, love bread and there is no quicker convenience food. Ring the changes with these super-speedy snacks.

Shape Sorters

Serves 2

4 slices bread
butter or margarine, for spreading
30ml/2 tbsp smooth peanut butter
50g/2oz/½ cup grated Cheddar cheese
4 cherry tomatoes
3 slices cucumber

VARIATION
Pizza Shape Sorters
Spread the shapes with tomato ketchup. Chop a tomato finely, and sprinkle over the shapes, then add some grated cheese. Grill until bubbly and golden.

1 Toast the bread lightly on both sides and remove crusts. Stamp out shapes using square, star, triangle and round.

2 Spread the shapes with butter or margarine and then peanut butter. Place the shapes on a baking sheet and sprinkle with cheese.

3 Grill until the cheese is bubbly. Cool slightly, arrange on a plate and serve with tomato wedges and quartered cucumber slices.

Happy Families

Serves 2

3 slices bread
butter or margarine, for spreading
3 slices processed cheese
2 slices ham
a little mustard and cress
1 strip red pepper
½ carrot
small pieces of cucumber

1 Stamp out men and women shapes from the bread using small cutters. Spread with a little butter or margarine.

2 Stamp out cheese dresses using the woman cutter and trimming off the head. Press on to three of the bodies. Cut out cheese jumpers and ham trousers and braces. Add to the remaining shapes.

3 Snip off the leaves from mustard and cress and use for eyes. Cut tiny red pepper mouths and make necklaces and bow ties from the carrot and cucumber using flower cutters. Arrange on plates.

Eggy Bread Butterflies

Serves 2

4 small broccoli florets
8 peas
1 small carrot
1 slice red Leicester or Cheddar cheese
2 slices ham
2 slices bread
1 egg
10ml/2 tsp milk
5ml/1 tsp sunflower oil
a little tomato ketchup

1 Cook the broccoli florets and the peas in a saucepan of boiling water for 5 minutes. Drain well.

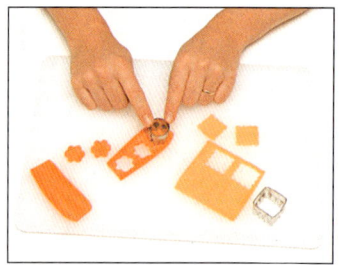

2 For each butterfly, cut four thin slices of carrot and cut into flower shapes with a petits four cutter. Cut out four small squares from the cheese.

3 Cut four thin strips from the rest of the carrot for antennae. Roll up each piece of ham and arrange in the middle of two serving plates, to make the two butterfly bodies.

4 Cut butterfly wings from the bread using a small knife.

5 Beat together the egg and milk and dip the bread in to coat both sides thoroughly. Heat the oil in a medium-sized frying pan and fry the bread until golden on both sides.

6 Assemble the butterfly, using the eggy bread for the wings and decorating with the carrot, cheese, broccoli and peas. Use a blob of ketchup for the head.

> **TIP**
> Vary the ingredients for butterfly decorations. Make a body from a grilled sausage if preferred.

Tuna Flowers

Serves 2–3

6 thin slices bread
25g/1oz butter, plus extra if necessary
10ml/2 tsp plain flour
75ml/5 tbsp milk
60ml/4 tbsp grated red Leicester or Cheddar cheese
100g/3½oz can tuna fish, drained
50g/2oz/4 tbsp frozen mixed vegetables, defrosted
½ carrot
6 slices cucumber, halved
a little mustard and cress
salt and pepper (optional)

1 Preheat the oven to 200°C/ 400°F/Gas 6. Cut out six flower shapes from the bread using a 9cm/ 3½in scalloped biscuit cutter. Flatten each piece slightly with a rolling pin.

2 Melt the butter in a saucepan or microwave. Brush a little over one side of each piece of bread and then press the bread, buttered side downwards, into sections of a bun tray. Brush the second side of bread with a little more butter.

3 Bake in the oven for about 10–12 minutes until crisp and golden around the edges.

4 Stir the flour into the remaining butter (you should have about 10ml/2 tsp left). Gradually stir in the milk and bring to the boil, stirring until the sauce is thick and smooth.

5 Stir in 30ml/3 tbsp of the cheese, the tuna, the mixed vegetables and a little salt and pepper, if liked.

6 Heat through and then spoon into the baked bread cups and sprinkle with remaining cheese.

7 Arrange the tuna cups on serving plates. Cut the carrot into thin strips for flower stems and add to the plate with halved cucumber slices for leaves and mustard and cress for grass.

Noughts and Crosses

Serves 2

8 green beans
¼ red pepper
6 slices snack pepperami sausage
2 slices bread
butter or margarine, for spreading
115g/4oz Cheddar cheese

TIP
To vary the topping, use thin strips of carrot or ham for the grid, sliced sausage, frankfurter or carrot for the noughts, carrot, green pepper or cucumber for the crosses.

1. Trim the beans, thinly slice the pepper, discarding any seeds and thinly slice the pepperami sausage.

2. Cook the beans in boiling water for 5 minutes. Toast the bread lightly on both sides and spread with butter or margarine. Thinly slice the cheese and place on the toast.

3. Drain the beans and arrange four on each piece of toast to form a grid. Add crosses made from pepper strips and noughts from pieces of the pepperami sausage.

4. Grill the toasts until the cheese is bubbly. Arrange on plates and cool slightly before serving.

Stripy Cheese on Toast

Serves 2

2 slices bread
butter or margarine, for spreading
50g/2oz Cheddar cheese
50g/2oz red Leicester cheese
2 cherry tomatoes, to serve

1. Toast the bread lightly on both sides then spread each slice with butter or margarine.

2. Thinly slice the cheese and then cut into strips about 2.5cm/1in wide. Arrange alternate coloured cheese strips over the toast and grill the toasts until bubbly.

3. Cool slightly, then cut into squares, arrange on plates and serve with cherry tomato wedges.

TIP
If your child likes Marmite add a thin scraping underneath the cheese slices. You could also spread ketchup or peanut butter for a surprise flavour.

Speedy Sausage Rolls

Makes 18

8 slices multi-grain white bread

225g/8oz cocktail sausages

40g/1½oz/3 tbsp butter or sunflower margarine

carrot and cucumber sticks, to serve

1 Preheat the oven to 190°C/ 375°F/Gas 5. Trim the crusts off the bread and cut into slices a little smaller than the sausages.

2 Wrap each piece of bread around a sausage and secure with a halved cocktail stick. Place the sausage rolls on a baking sheet.

3 Melt the butter or margarine in a small saucepan or in the microwave and brush over the prepared sausage rolls.

4 Bake in the oven for 15 minutes until browned. Cool slightly and remove the cocktail sticks. Arrange on a plate and serve with carrot and cucumber sticks.

TIP
If liked spread a little tomato relish or ketchup over the bread before wrapping around the sausages to give a sharper flavour. Spread the bread with a little mild, prepared mustard if you child likes it. If the bread is thickly cut, flatten it slightly with a rolling pin, before wrapping around the sausages.

Pizza Clock

Serves 3–4

20cm/8in ready-made pizza base
45ml/3 tbsp tomato ketchup or pizza sauce
2 tomatoes
75g/3oz/¾ cup grated cheese
pinch of dried marjoram
1 green pepper
1 large carrot
1 thick slice ham

3 Meanwhile halve the pepper, cut away the core and seeds and stamp out the numbers 3, 6, 9 and 12 with small number cutters. Peel and thinly cut the carrot lengthways and stamp out the numbers 1, 2, 4, 5, 7, 8, 10 and 11. Arrange on the pizza to form a clock face.

4 Cut out a carrot circle. Cut two clock hands, each about 7.5cm/3in long from the ham. Arrange on the pizza with the round of carrot.

5 Place the pizza clock on to a serving plate and arrange the numbers around the edge. Cool the pizza clock slightly before cutting into wedges and serving.

1 Preheat oven to 220°C/425°F/Gas 7. Place the pizza base on a baking sheet and spread with ketchup or pizza sauce. Chop the tomatoes and scatter over the pizza with the cheese and marjoram.

2 Place directly on an oven shelf and bake for 12 minutes, until the cheese is bubbly. (Place a baking tray on the shelf below the pizza to catch any drips of cheese.)

TIP
If preferred, make a smaller version of this using half a toasted muffin. Top as above and grill until the cheese melts. Add ham hands and small pieces of carrot to mark the numbers.

Spotty Sandwiches

Serves 2

1 hard-boiled egg
30ml/2 tbsp mayonnaise
2 slices white bread
2 slices brown bread
a little mustard and cress
½ small carrot
a little shredded lettuce

1 Peel and finely chop the egg, place in a small bowl and blend well with the mayonnaise.

2 Stamp out giraffe shapes from the brown and white bread using an animal biscuit cutter.

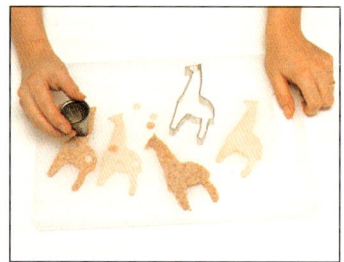

3 Cut tiny rounds from each shape using the end of a metal piping tube and then replace the rounds with opposite coloured bread circles.

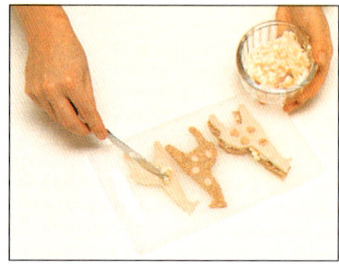

4 Spread the egg mayonnaise over half of the shapes and top with the remaining shapes. Arrange on plates with snipped mustard and cress for grass and shaped carrot slices for flowers.

Sandwich Snails

Serves 2

1 strip red pepper
small piece cucumber
15ml/1 tbsp frozen sweetcorn, defrosted
25g/1oz/¼ cup grated Cheddar cheese
15ml/1 tbsp mayonnaise
1 slice bread
2 cooked sausages

1 Cut away any seeds from the pepper and cut out four small squares for the snails' eyes and cut four strips of cucumber for their antennae. Finely chop the remaining pepper and cucumber and mix with the sweetcorn, cheese and mayonnaise. Place in a bowl.

2 Trim the crusts off the bread, cut in half and overlap two short edges together to make a long strip. Flatten slightly with a rolling pin so that the bread bonds together.

VARIATION
For pasta snails, use large shell pasta instead of the bread and stuff with the sweetcorn mixture.

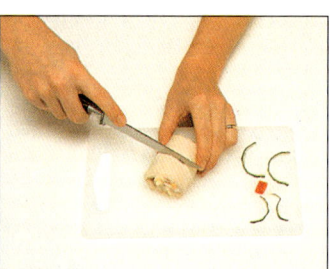

3 Spread the bread with the cheese mixture and roll up tightly. Squeeze together then cut in half crossways to make two rounds.

4 Arrange each slice, cut side uppermost, on two serving plates. Arrange the sausages for bodies, and use the cucumber strips for antennae and the red pepper squares for the eyes.

Easy Peasy Puds

With a young family to feed, puddings need to be quick, light and taste good without the kids realizing they're healthy too! Remember to keep sugar to a minimum.

Fruit Fondue

Serves 2

150g/5oz tub ready-to-serve low-fat custard
25g/1oz milk chocolate
1 eating apple
1 banana
1 satsuma
a few strawberries or seedless grapes

1. Pour the custard into a saucepan, add the chocolate and heat, stirring all the time until the chocolate has melted. Cool slightly.

2. Quarter the apple, core and cut into bite-sized pieces, slice the banana and break the satsuma into segments. Hull the strawberries and wash the grapes, if using.

3. Arrange the fruit on two small plates, pour the custard into two small dishes and place on the plates. The fruit can be dipped into the custard using either a fork or fingers.

TIP
Add the chocolate to a tub of custard and microwave on Full Power (100%) for 1½ minutes or until the chocolate has melted. Stir and spoon into dishes. Cool slightly.

Apple and Orange Fool

Makes: 250ml/8fl oz/1 cup

2 dessert apples
5ml/1 tsp grated orange rind and 15ml/1 tbsp orange juice
15ml/1 tbsp custard powder
5ml/1 tsp caster sugar
150ml/¼ pint/⅔ cup formula milk

1 Quarter, core and peel the apples. Slice and place the apples in a saucepan with the orange rind and juice.

2 Cover and cook gently for 10 minutes, stirring occasionally until the apples are soft.

3 Blend the custard powder and sugar with a little of the milk to make a smooth paste. Bring the remaining milk to the boil and stir into the custard mixture.

4 Return the custard to the pan and slowly bring to the boil, stirring until thickened and smooth.

5 Process or mash the apple to the desired consistency. Add the custard and stir to mix.

6 Spoon a little into a bowl, test the temperature and cool if necessary, before serving.

7 Cover the remaining fool and transfer to the fridge as soon as possible. Use within 24 hours.

- Suitable for freezing.

Peach Melba Dessert

Makes: 175ml/6fl oz/¾ cup

1 ripe peach

25g/1oz fresh or frozen raspberries

15ml/1 tbsp icing sugar

115g/4oz natural Greek yogurt

VARIATION
Bananarama
To make a single portion, use ½ a small banana and 15ml/1 tbsp of natural Greek yogurt. Mash the banana until smooth and add the yogurt. Stir to mix and serve immediately. Do not make this dessert in advance, as the banana will discolour while standing.

4 Set aside to cool then stir in the sugar and swirl in the yogurt. Spoon a little into a dish.

5 Cover the remaining dessert and transfer to the fridge. Use within 24 hours.

1 Halve the peach, discard the stone then peel and slice. Place in a saucepan with the raspberries and 15ml/1 tbsp water.

2 Cover and cook gently for 10 minutes until soft.

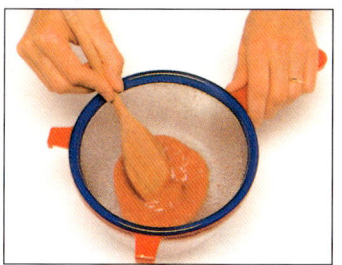

3 Purée and press through a sieve to remove the raspberry pips.

TIP
The finished pudding is not suitable for freezing although the sweetened fruit purée can be frozen successfully in sections of an ice cube tray. Defrost cubes of purée and mix each cube with 15ml/ 1 tbsp yogurt.

Strawberry Ice Cream

Makes 900ml/1½ pint/3¾ cups

300ml/½ pint/1¼ cups double cream

425g/15oz can custard

450g/1lb strawberries

teddy bear wafers, to decorate

strawberries, to decorate

1 Whip the cream until softly peaking then fold in the custard.

2 Hull the strawberries and then rinse and pat dry. Process to make a smooth purée, then press through a sieve into the cream and custard. Fold together.

3 Pour the mixture into a plastic tub and freeze the ice cream for 6–7 hours until half frozen.

4 Beat the ice cream with a fork or process in a food blender until smooth, then return the tub to the freezer and freeze until solid.

5 Remove the ice cream from the freezer 10 minutes before serving so that it can soften slightly. Scoop into serving bowls and decorate each with teddy bear wafers and extra fruit such as strawberries.

VARIATIONS
Strawberry Ripple Ice Cream
Purée and sieve an extra 250g/9oz strawberries and sweeten with 30ml/ 2 tbsp icing sugar. Swirl this into the half-frozen ice cream at Step 4 and then freeze until solid.

Apricot and Chocolate Chip Ice Cream
Whisk 300ml/½ pint/1¼ cups double cream, and fold in 425g/15oz can custard. Drain and purée the contents of a 425g/15oz can apricot slices in natural juice and stir into the cream with the finely grated rind of 1 orange. Pour into a plastic tub, freeze until mushy and then beat well. Stir in 100g/3½oz packet chocolate dots and freeze again until solid. Scoop into serving dishes and decorate the ice cream with orange segments and wafers, if liked.

Raspberry Sorbet

Makes: 900ml/1½ pints/3¾ cups

| 10ml/2 tsp powdered gelatine |
| 600ml/1 pint/2½ cups water |
| 225g/8oz/1¼ cups caster sugar |
| 675g/1½lb raspberries, hulled |
| grated rind and juice of ½ lemon |

1 Put 30ml/2 tbsp water in a cup, sprinkle the gelatine over and set aside for a few minutes to soak.

2 Place the water and sugar in a saucepan and heat, stirring occasionally until the sugar has completely dissolved.

3 Bring to the boil and boil rapidly for 3 minutes. Remove from the heat, add the gelatine mixture to the syrup and stir until completely dissolved. Leave to cool.

4 Liquidize or process the raspberries to a smooth purée then press through a sieve into the syrup. Stir in lemon rind and juice.

5 Pour into a plastic tub and freeze for 6–7 hours or until the mixture is half frozen.

6 Beat the sorbet with a fork or transfer to a food processor and process until smooth. Return to the freezer and freeze until solid.

7 Remove the sorbet from the freezer 10 minutes before serving to soften slightly, then scoop into dishes with a melon baller or small teaspoon.

VARIATION
Summer Fruit Sorbet
Follow the recipe up to Step 3. Put a 500g/1¼lb pack of frozen summer fruits into a second saucepan. Add 60ml/4 tbsp water, cover and cook for 5 minutes until soft, then purée and sieve, add to the syrup and continue as above.

Yogurt Lollies

Makes 6

150g/5oz tub strawberry yogurt

150ml/¼ pint/⅔ cup milk

10ml/2 tsp strawberry milkshake powder

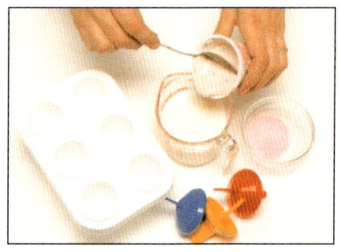

2 Pour the mixture into six small plastic lolly moulds. Add the lolly handles and freeze overnight.

3 Dip the lolly moulds into hot water, count to 15, then flex handles and remove. Serve at once.

1 Mix the yogurt, milk and milkshake powder together.

TIP
Store lollies for up to a week in the freezer. Make sure they are tightly covered as they can pick up other flavours in the freezer.

Jolly Jellies

Serves 4

150g/5oz packet strawberry jelly

2 ripe plums

175g/6oz fromage frais or Greek yogurt

4 Dolly Mixtures

10ml/2 tsp sugar or chocolate strands

2 Halve the plums, cut away the stones and reserve four thin slices. Chop the remaining fruit and divide among four small dishes.

3 Stir the fromage frais into the jelly and pour into the dishes. Chill in the refrigerator until set.

4 Decorate with sliced plums for mouths, halved dolly mixtures for the eyes and sugar or chocolate sugar strands for hair.

1 Cut the jelly into pieces. Place in a bowl and pour over 150ml/ ¼ pint/⅔ cup boiling water. Stir until dissolved then set aside to cool.

TIP
If you have a fussy eater who hates bits, finely chop or purée the plums before adding to the jelly so that the child doesn't know it's not just jelly!

Pancakes

Serves 2–3

| 50g/2oz/⅓ cup plain flour |
| 1 egg |
| 150ml/¼ pint/⅔ cup milk |
| 15ml/1 tbsp sunflower oil |

For the filling

| 1 banana |
| 1 orange |
| 2–3 scoops ice cream |
| a little maple syrup |

1 Sift the flour into a bowl, add the egg and gradually whisk in the milk to form a smooth batter. Whisk in 5ml/1 tsp of the oil.

2 To make the filling, slice the banana thinly or in chunks. Cut the peel away from the orange with a serrated knife, then cut the orange into segments.

3 Heat a little of the remaining oil in medium-sized non-stick pan, pour off any excess oil and add 30ml/2 tbsp of the batter. Tilt the pan to evenly coat the pan and cook for a couple of minutes until the pancake is set and the underside is golden.

4 Loosen the edges with a knife then toss the pancake or turn with a knife. Brown the other side and then slide out on to a plate. Fold in four and keep warm.

5 Cook the rest of the batter in the same way until you have made 6 pancakes. Place two on each plate.

6 Spoon a little fruit into each pancake and arrange on serving plates. Top with the remaining fruit, a scoop of ice cream and pour over a little maple syrup. Serve at once.

Traffic Light Sundaes

Serves 6

½ packet lime jelly
½ packet orange jelly
½ packet strawberry jelly
2 kiwi fruit
275g/10oz can mandarin oranges
6 scoops vanilla ice cream, to serve
12 strawberries to decorate

4 Add a little kiwi fruit and continue making layers using the orange jelly and mandarins and topping with the strawberry jelly.

5 Add half the strawberries, top with a scoop of ice cream and decorate with the remaining strawberries. Serve immediately.

1 Make up each jelly in a separate bowl with boiling water according to the instructions on the packet. Cool, then transfer to the fridge and allow to set.

2 Peel and slice the kiwi fruit, hull and rinse the strawberries and cut in half. Drain the mandarins.

3 Chop all of the jellies and divide the green jelly equally among six sundae glasses.

TIP
This is a great recipe for a party tea – simple but ever popular. For smaller numbers of children, halve the recipe to make three. Or for tiny children make up half-size sundaes in plastic cups.

Cheat's Trifle

Serves 2

2 slices Swiss roll

20ml/4 tsp orange juice

1 mandarin orange

50g/2oz strawberries

150g/5oz tub ready-to-serve custard

10ml/2 tsp Greek yogurt

2 sugar flowers, to decorate

> **TIP**
> Use 150ml/¼ pint/⅔ cup leftover custard if you have it or make custard with custard powder and 150ml/¼ pint/⅔ cup milk.

1 Put a slice of Swiss roll in the base of two ramekin dishes and spoon the orange juice over the top. Peel the mandarin orange and divide the segments between the dishes.

2 Hull, rinse and chop the strawberries. Place in dishes.

3 Spoon the custard over the strawberries, top with yogurt and decorate with sugar flowers.

Baked Bananas

Serves 2

2 medium bananas

2 small scoops ice cream

1 Preheat the oven to 180°C/350°F/Gas 4. Separate the unpeeled bananas and put on a baking sheet. Cook for 10 minutes until the skins have blackened and the bananas feel quite soft.

2 Hold the banana in a tea cloth, make a slit along the length of the banana and peel off the skin. Peel the second banana.

3 Slice and arrange each as a ring on a plate. Place a scoop of ice cream in the centre of each plate.

> **TIP**
> For an adult version, slit the banana and spoon in a teaspoon or two of coffee cream liqueur, eat out of the skin with a teaspoon.

Quick Cakes and Bakes the Kids can Make

Cooking is fun and the earlier you learn the better fun it is. Even the faddiest eater can be an enthusiastic cook, and helping to decide what to cook for tea can make a child more willing to sit down with the family and hand round their homemade goodies. Learning to weigh out ingredients, to mix, spread and spoon out, all helps with co-ordination and encourages a basic interest and love of food.

Getting ready
- Find a large apron or cover the child's clothes with an old adult-sized shirt with the sleeves cut down.
- Always wash hands before you start to cook.

- Choose a sturdy chair for your child to stand on next to the work top or kitchen table. Or put a large cloth on the floor, set scales, bowls, ingredients etc out, and prepare food sitting down.

- Make it clear to your child that only the adult opens the oven door and touches saucepans on the cooker.
- Keep knives and scissors out of the way; provide blunt, round-ended scissors if required.

Orange and Apple Rockies

Makes 24

oil, for greasing
115g/4oz/½ cup sunflower margarine
225g/8oz/2 cups self-raising flour
1 large eating apple
50g/2oz ready-to-eat dried apricots
grated rind of 1 small orange
75g/3oz/⅓ cup demerara sugar
1 egg
15ml/1 tbsp milk
apple slices, to serve

1 Preheat the oven to 190°C/375°F/Gas 5 and brush two baking sheets with a little oil. Rub the margarine into the flour with your fingertips until the mixture resembles fine breadcrumbs.

2 Peel, core and finely chop the apple, chop the apricots and stir into the flour mixture with the sultanas and orange rind. Reserve 30ml/2 tbsp of the sugar and stir the rest into the mixture.

3 Beat the egg and milk, add to the flour mixture and mix until just beginning to bind together.

4 Drop spoonfuls, well spaced apart on to the baking sheet. Sprinkle with the reserved sugar and bake in the oven for 12–15 minutes. Transfer to a serving plate and serve warm or cold with apple slices.

TIP
Freeze any leftover rockies in a plastic bag for up to three months.

Mini Cup Cakes

Makes: 26

50g/2oz/4 tbsp soft margarine

50g/2oz/¼ cup caster sugar

50g/2oz/⅓ cup self-raising flour

1 egg

1. Preheat the oven to 180°C/350°F/Gas 4. Separate 26 paper mini muffin cases and place on a large baking sheet.

2. Put all the ingredients for the cake into a mixing bowl and beat together well until smooth.

3. Divide the mixture among the cases and cook for 8–10 minutes until well risen and golden.

4. Transfer cakes to a wire rack and leave to cool completely, then peel the paper off one or two cakes and serve.

5. Store the remaining cakes in a plastic box for up to three days.

• Suitable for freezing up to three months in a plastic box.

TIP
Cut a cup cake in half crossways and spread one half with a little sugar-free jam. Replace top half and serve.

Shortbread Shapes

Makes: 60

little oil, for greasing

150g/5oz/1 cup plain flour

25g/1oz/3 tbsp cornflour

50g/2oz/¼ cup caster sugar

115g/4oz/½ cup butter

extra sugar, for sprinkling (optional)

1 Preheat the oven to 180°C/350°F/Gas 4. Brush two baking sheets with a little oil.

2 Put the flour, cornflour and sugar in a bowl. Cut the butter into pieces and rub into the flour until the mixture resembles fine breadcrumbs. Mould to a dough with your hands.

3 Knead lightly and roll out on a floured surface to a 5mm/¼in thickness. Stamp out shapes with small biscuit or petits fours cutters.

4 Transfer to the baking sheets, sprinkle with extra sugar, if liked, and cook for 10–12 minutes until pale golden. Loosen with a knife and leave to cool on the baking sheets, then transfer to a wire rack.

5 Offer your child one or two shapes and store the rest in a plastic box for up to one week.

TIP
These biscuits will keep well in the freezer for three months. Pack in rigid plastic boxes and thaw in a single layer. If you prefer, you can freeze the biscuits before baking. Wrap well to prevent them taking up flavours from other food.

Date Crunch

Makes 24 pieces

225g/8oz packet sweetmeal biscuits
75g/3oz stoned dates
75g/3oz/⅓ cup butter
30ml/2 tbsp golden syrup
75g/3oz sultanas
150g/5oz milk or dark chocolate

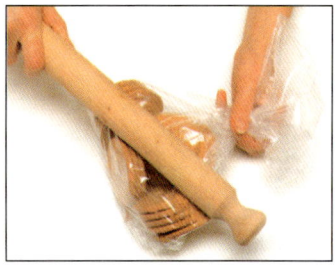

1. Line an 18cm/7in shallow tin with foil. Put the biscuits in a plastic bag and crush roughly with a rolling pin. Finely chop the dates.

2. Gently heat the butter and syrup in a small saucepan until the butter has melted.

TIP
For an alternative topping drizzle 75g/3oz melted white and 75g/3oz melted dark chocolate over the biscuit to give random squiggly lines. Chill until set.

3. Stir in the crushed biscuits, the dates and sultanas and mix well. Spoon into the tin, press flat with the back of a spoon and chill for 1 hour.

4. Break the chocolate into a bowl, melt over hot water, and then spoon over the biscuit mixture spreading evenly with a palette knife. Chill until set.

5. Lift the foil out of the tin and peel away. Cut the biscuit into 24 pieces and arrange on a plate.

Chocolate Dominoes

Makes 16

oil, for greasing
175g/6oz/¾ cup soft margarine
175g/6oz/⅞ cup caster sugar
150g/5oz/⅔ cup self-raising flour
25g/1oz cocoa powder, sifted
3 eggs

For the Topping
175g/6oz/¾ cup butter, softened
25g/1oz cocoa powder
300g/11oz/3 cups icing sugar
a few liquorice strips and 115g/4oz packet M & M's, for decoration

1 Preheat the oven to 180°C/350°F/Gas 4. Lightly brush an 18 × 28cm/7 × 11in baking tin with a little oil and line the base of the tin with greaseproof paper.

2 Put all the cake ingredients in a bowl and beat until smooth.

3 Spoon into the tin and level the surface with a palette knife.

4 Bake in the oven for 30 minutes, or until the cake springs back when pressed with the fingertips.

5 Cool in the tin for 5 minutes, then loosen the edges with a knife and turn out on to a wire rack. Peel off the paper and allow the cake to cool.

6 Turn the cake on to a chopping board and cut into 16 bars.

7 To make the topping, place the butter in a bowl, sift in the cocoa and icing sugar and beat until smooth. Spread the topping evenly over the cakes with a palette knife.

8 Add a strip of liquorice to each cake, decorate with M & M's for domino dots and arrange the cakes on a serving plate.

VARIATION
Traffic Light Cakes
Makes 16
To make Traffic Light Cakes omit the cocoa and add an extra 25g/1oz/3 tbsp flour. Omit the cocoa from the icing and add an extra 25g/1oz/3 tbsp icing sugar and flavour with 2.5ml/½ tsp vanilla essence. Spread over the cakes and decorate with eight halved red, yellow and green glacé cherries to look like traffic lights. Arrange the cakes on a serving plate.

Marshmallow Krispie Cakes

Makes 45

oil, for greasing
250g/9oz bag toffees
50g/2oz/4 tbsp butter
45ml/3 tbsp milk
115g/4oz marshmallows
175g/6oz Rice Krispies

1 Lightly brush a 20 × 33cm/8 × 13in roasting tin with a little oil. Put the toffees, butter and milk in a saucepan and heat gently, stirring until the toffees have melted.

2 Add the marshmallows and cereal and stir until well mixed and the marshmallows have melted.

3 Spoon into the tin, level the surface and leave to set. Cut into squares, put into paper cases and serve.

Mini Muffins

Makes 24

200g/7oz/1½ cups plain flour
10ml/2 tsp baking powder
50g/2oz/¼ cup soft light brown sugar
150ml/¼ pint/⅔ cup milk
1 egg, beaten
50g/2oz/4 tbsp butter or margarine, melted
50g/2oz glacé cherries
50g/2oz ready-to-eat dried apricots
2.5ml/½ tsp vanilla essence

1 Preheat the oven to 220°C/425°F/Gas 7 and place 24 petits fours cases in the sections of two petits fours, or mini muffin tins.

TIP
For older children spoon the mixture into 12 medium-sized muffin cases. Muffins are best served warm from the oven. If they don't get eaten straight away, they can be frozen for up to three months.

2 Place the flour, baking powder and sugar in a bowl and add the milk, egg and melted butter or margarine and stir thoroughly until the mixture is smooth.

3 Chop the cherries and apricots and stir into the muffin mixture with the vanilla essence.

VARIATIONS
Chocolate Chip Muffins
Substitute 25g/1oz cocoa powder for 25g/1oz/2 tbsp flour. Omit the cherries, apricots and vanilla and add 50g/2oz white and 50g/2oz plain chocolate dots.

4 Spoon the muffin mixture into the paper cases so they are about three-quarters full.

5 Cook for 10–12 minutes until well risen and browned. If you have just one tin cook in two batches.

Orange and Banana Muffins
Substitute 2 small mashed bananas for 60ml/2fl oz/¼ cup milk. Omit the cherries, apricot and vanilla and add 15ml/1 tbsp grated orange rind.

Cup Cake Faces

Makes 12

115g/4oz/⅔ cup sunflower margarine
115g/4oz/⅔ cup caster sugar
115g/4oz/1 cup self-raising flour
2 eggs

For the Topping
50g/2oz/¼ cup butter
115g/4oz/1 cup icing sugar
pink food colouring
115g/4oz packet M & M's
2 red liquorice bootlaces
12 Dolly Mixtures
75g/3oz plain chocolate

1 Preheat the oven to 180°C/350°F/Gas 4. Place 12 paper cake cases in the sections of a bun tray.

2 Put all the cake ingredients into a bowl and beat until smooth.

3 Divide the cake mixture among the cases and cook for 12–15 minutes until well risen and the cakes spring back when pressed with a fingertip. Leave to cool.

4 Meanwhile make the topping: beat the butter in a bowl, sift in the icing sugar and beat the mixture until smooth. Stir in a little pink food colouring.

5 Spread the icing over the cakes. Add M & M eyes, short pieces of liquorice for mouths and a dolly mixture nose.

6 Break the chocolate into pieces, melt in a bowl over a saucepan of gently simmering water and then spoon into a greaseproof paper piping bag. Snip off the tip and pipe hair, eye balls, glasses and moustaches on to the cakes.

7 Carefully arrange in a single layer on a serving plate and allow the icing to set before serving.

VARIATION
Alphabet Cakes
Make up a half quantity of cake mixture as above and spoon into 24 mini muffin or petits fours cases. Put into sections of a mini muffin or petits fours tin or arrange on a baking sheet close together and cook for 8–10 minutes then cool. Blend 225g/8oz/2 cups sifted icing sugar with 30ml/2 tbsp water until smooth. Add a little water if necessary to make a thick spoonable icing. Spoon 30ml/2 tbsp into a piping bag fitted with a small writing tube. Spoon half the remaining icing into a separate bowl and colour pink. Colour the remaining icing blue. Spoon the icing over the cakes, smooth the surface and pipe on letters of the alphabet. Leave to set.

Gingerbread People

Makes 24

oil, for greasing
225g/8oz/2 cups plain flour
5ml/1 tsp ground ginger
1.5ml/¼ tsp ground cinnamon
7.5ml/1½ tsp bicarbonate of soda
50g/2oz/4 tbsp sunflower margarine
115g/4oz/⅔ cup soft light brown sugar
45ml/3 tbsp golden syrup
30ml/2 tbsp milk
75g/3oz dark chocolate
2 packets M & M's

1 Brush two baking sheets with a little oil. Sift the flour, spices and bicarbonate of soda into a bowl.

2 Place the margarine, sugar and syrup in a saucepan and heat until the margarine has melted.

3 Remove from heat and stir in the flour mixture and milk. Mix to a firm dough, chill for 30 minutes.

TIP
Chocolate decorations soften biscuits, so eat on the day or decorate as many biscuits as you will eat and store the rest in a tin for up to four days. For a party, decorate people with clothes cut from coloured ready-to-roll icing.

4 Preheat the oven to 160°C/325°F/Gas 3. Knead the dough lightly and roll out on a floured surface. Cut out gingerbread men and women with 9cm/3½in cutters. Place on the baking sheets, reroll the trimmings, stamp out nine gingerbread people and continue until all the dough is used.

5 Cook for 10 minutes until golden and then set aside to cool and harden a little on the trays. Loosen while still warm.

6 Break the chocolate into a bowl and melt over hot water, then spoon a little chocolate over the gingerbread men for trousers. Place on the baking tray to set.

7 Spoon the remaining chocolate into a piping bag fitted with a small writing tube and pipe faces on the gingerbread people and some swirls for petticoats on the women. Pipe two dots on all the people for buttons and stick on M & M's. Leave to set before serving.

Bread Animals

Makes 15

oil, for greasing
2 × 280g/10oz packets white bread mix
a few currants
½ small red pepper
1 small carrot
1 egg

1 Brush two large baking sheets with a little oil. Put the bread mixes in a large bowl and make up as directed on the packet with warm water.

2 Knead on a lightly floured surface for 5 minutes until the dough is smooth and elastic. Return the dough to the bowl, cover with oiled clear film and leave in a warm place for ¾–1 hour until it has doubled in size.

3 Preheat the oven to 220°C/425°F/Gas 7. Knead the dough again for 5 minutes and then divide into five pieces.

4 To make snakes, take one piece of dough, cut into three and shape each into a 15cm/6in snake, making a slit in one end for the mouth. Twist the snakes on the baking sheet. Insert two currants for eyes. Cut out a thin strip of pepper, cutting a triangle at one end for the forked tongue.

5 For hedgehogs, take another piece of dough and cut into three. Shape each into an oval about 6cm/2½in long. Place on the baking sheet and add currant eyes and a red pepper nose. Snip the dough with scissors to make the prickly spines.

6 For the mice, take a third piece of dough and cut into four pieces. Shape three pieces into ovals each about 6cm/2½in long and place on the baking sheet. Shape tiny rounds of dough for ears and wiggly tails from the fourth piece of dough. Press onto the mice bodies and use the currants for eyes.

7 Cut small strips of carrot and use for whiskers.

TIP
Give a portion of the prepared dough to your children, with some chopped dried fruits and allow them to create their very own Bread Animals.

8 For the crocodiles, cut another piece of dough into three. Take a small piece off each and reserve. Shape the large pieces into 10cm/4in long sausages. Make slits for the mouths and wedge open with crumpled foil. Add currant eyes. Shape the spare dough into feet and press into position. Make criss-cross cuts on the backs.

9 For rabbits, take the final piece of dough and cut into three. Take a small piece off each for tails. Roll the remaining pieces of dough into thick sausages 18cm/7in long. Loop the dough and twist twice to form the body and head of rabbit. Use the rest for tails.

10 Cover the shapes with oiled clear film and leave in a warm place for 10–15 minutes. Brush with beaten egg and cook for 10–12 minutes until golden.

11 Serve warm or cold split and filled with ham or cheese.

Cheesy Shapes

Makes 15

oil, for greasing
350g/12oz/3 cups self-raising flour
pinch of salt
115g/4oz/½ cup sunflower margarine
115g/4oz Cheddar cheese
2 eggs, beaten
60ml/4 tbsp milk
10ml/2 tsp sesame seeds
10ml/2 tsp poppy seeds

1. Preheat the oven to 220°C/ 425°F/Gas 7.

2. Place the flour and salt in a bowl, add the margarine and rub in with your fingertips or an electric mixer until the mixture resembles fine breadcrumbs.

3. Grate the cheese, reserve 30ml/ 2 tbsp and stir the rest into the flour. Add three-quarters of the beaten eggs and milk to the flour and mix to a soft dough.

4. Knead the dough lightly and roll out thickly on a surface that has been dusted with flour.

5. Stamp out numbers with 7cm/3in cutters and arrange well spaced apart on two baking sheets. Reroll trimmings and stamp out more shapes to use up the pastry.

6. Brush the tops of the numbers with the reserved egg. Sprinkle five of the numbers with sesame seeds, five with poppy seeds and the remainder with grated cheese.

7. Cook for 12–15 minutes until well risen and browned. Cool slightly then arrange the Cheesy Shapes on a plate and serve warm.

Marmite and Cheese Whirls

Makes 16

oil, for greasing

250g/9oz frozen puff pastry, defrosted

flour, for dusting

2.5ml/½ tsp Marmite

1 egg, beaten

50g/2oz red Leicester or Cheddar cheese, grated

carrot and cucumber sticks, to serve

1 Preheat the oven to 220°C/425°F/Gas 7 and brush a large baking sheet with a little oil.

2 Roll out the pastry on a floured surface to a large rectangle, about 35.5 × 25cm/14 × 10in.

3 Spread the pastry with Marmite, leaving a 1cm/½in border. Brush the edges of the pastry with egg and sprinkle the cheese to cover the Marmite.

4 Roll the pastry up quite tightly like a Swiss roll, starting from a longer edge. Brush the outside of the pastry with beaten egg.

5 Cut the roll into thick slices and place on the baking sheet.

6 Cook for 12–15 minutes until the pastry is well risen and golden. Arrange on a serving plate and serve warm or cold with carrot and cucumber sticks.

TIP
Omit the Marmite and use peanut butter if preferred. If the shapes become a little squashed when sliced, reform into rounds by opening out the layers with the end of a knife.

INDEX

A
Apples
  apple and orange fool, 70
  fruit fondue, 68
  orange and apple rockies, 80
  sticky ribs and apple slaw, 30
Apricots
  apricot and chocolate chip ice cream, 72
  mini muffins, 86
Aubergines
  aubergine bolognese, 41
  vegetable lasagne, 40

B
Baked beans
  cowboy bangers and beans, 26
  Mexican mince, 20
Balanced diet, 8
Bananas
  baked bananas, 78
  bananarama, 71
  fruit fondue, 68
  orange and banana muffins, 86
  pancakes, 76
Batter
  mini toad-in-the-hole, 26
Bean sprouts
  pick-up sticks, 32
Beef
  beef and mushroom burgers, 54
  cannibal necklaces, 53
  Mexican mince, 20
  peppered beef casserole, 18
  shepherd's pie, 22
Biscuits
  date crunch, 84
Bread
  bread animals, 90
  eggy bread butterflies, 60
  happy families, 58
  noughts and crosses, 62
  sandwich snails, 66
  shape sorters, 58
  speedy sausage rolls, 64
  spotty sandwiches, 66
  stripy cheese on toast, 62
  tuna flowers, 61
Breakfast, importance of, 8
Broccoli
  broccoli and cauliflower cheese, 35
  eggy bread butterflies, 60
  fat cats, 37
  veggie burgers, 38

C
Cabbage
  cheesy fish pies, 24
  fish finger log cabins, 56
  sticky ribs and apple slaw, 30
Cakes
  alphabet cakes, 88
  chocolate chip muffins, 86
  chocolate dominoes, 85
  cup cake faces, 88
  gingerbread people, 89
  marshmallow krispie cakes, 86
  mini cup cakes, 82
  mini muffins, 86
  orange and apple rockies, 80
  orange and banana muffins, 86
  traffic light cakes, 85
Cannibal necklaces, 53
Carrots
  pick-up sticks, 32
  potato, carrot and courgette rosti, 38
  vegetable lasagne, 40
  veggie burgers, 38
Casseroles and stews
  coriander chicken casserole, 16
  lamb and celery casserole, 20
  lamb stew, 19
  peppered beef casserole, 18
  pork and lentil casserole, 29
Cauliflower
  broccoli and cauliflower cheese, 35
Celery
  lamb and celery casserole, 20
  pick-up sticks, 32
  speedy chicken pie, 42
Cheat's trifle, 78
Cheese
  broccoli and cauliflower cheese, 35
  cheesy chicken parcels, 16
  cheesy fish pies, 24
  cheesy shapes, 92
  eggy bread butterflies, 60
  fat cats, 37
  ham salad clown, 46
  happy families, 58
  Marmite and cheese whirls, 93
  Mexican mince, 20
  mini cheese and ham tarts, 31
  noughts and crosses, 62
  pizza clocks, 64
  potato boats, 36
  sandwich snails, 86
  saucy ham pasta, 49
  saucy spinach pancakes, 34
  shape sorters, 58
  skinny dippers, 44
  speedy chicken pie, 42
  stripy cheese on toast, 62
  tuna flowers, 61
  vegetable lasagne, 40
Chicken
  cheesy chicken parcels, 16
  coriander chicken casserole, 16
  skinny dippers, 44
  speedy chicken pie, 42
  sweet and sour chicken, 45
Chips
  skinny dippers, 44
  Spanish omelette, 48
Chocolate
  apricot and chocolate chip ice cream, 72
  chocolate chip muffins, 86
  chocolate dominoes, 85
  date crunch, 84
  fruit fondue, 68
Cod
  four fast fishes, 55
Coriander
  coriander chicken casserole, 16
Corned beef hash, 52
Courgettes
  potato, carrot and courgette rosti, 38
  vegetable lasagne, 40
Couscous
  peppered beef casserole, 18
Cowboy bangers and beans, 26
Custard
  apple and orange fool, 70
  cheat's trifle, 78
  fruit fondue, 68
  strawberry ice cream, 72

D
Dates
  date crunch, 84

E
Eating together, 12

INDEX

Eggs
  eggy bread
    butterflies, 60
  ham and tomato
    scramble, 46
  Spanish omelette, 48
  spotty sandwiches,
    66

F
Fat cats, 37
Fats, 9
Fish finger log cabins,
  56
Food fads, 7
Fromage frais
  jolly jellies, 74
Fruit, 9
  fruit fondue, 68
  summer fruit sorbet,
    73
Fussy eaters, 10–13

G
Gingerbread people, 89
Green beans
  noughts and crosses,
    62
  pick-up sticks, 32
  tuna fish cakes, 23

H
Ham
  cheesy chicken
    parcels, 16
  eggy bread
    butterflies, 60
  ham and tomato
    scramble, 46
  ham salad clown, 46
  happy families, 58
  mini cheese and ham
    tarts, 31
  pizza clocks, 64
  potato boats, 36
  quickie kebabs, 50
  saucy ham pasta, 49
  sausage wrappers, 50
  Spanish omelette, 48
Hoki
  cheesy fish pies, 24
  four fast fishes, 55

I
Ice cream
  apricot and chocolate
    chip ice cream, 72
  baked bananas, 78
  strawberry ice cream,
    72
  traffic light sundaes,
    77

J
Jelly
  jolly jellies, 74
  traffic light sundaes,
    77

K
Kebabs
  quickie kebabs, 50
Kidney beans
  peppered beef
    casserole, 18
Kiwi fruit
  traffic light sundaes,
    77

L
Lamb
  lamb and celery
    casserole, 20
  lamb stew, 19
Leeks
  aubergine bolognese,
    41
  pick-up sticks, 32
  potato boats, 35
Lentils
  aubergine bolognese,
    41
  pork and lentil
    casserole, 29

M
Marmite
  Marmite and cheese
    whirls, 93
Marshmallow krispie
  cakes, 86
Mexican mince, 20
Mini cheese and ham
  tarts, 31
Mini toad-in-the-hole,
  26

Muffins
  chocolate chip
    muffins, 86
  mini muffins, 86
  orange and banana
    muffins, 86
Mushrooms
  beef and mushroom
    burgers, 54
  potato boats, 36
  quickie kebabs, 50

O
Oranges
  apple and orange
    fool, 70
  fruit fondue, 68
  orange and apple
    rockies, 80
  orange and banana
    muffins, 86
  pancakes, 76
  traffic light sundaes,
    77

P
Pancakes
  saucy spinach
    pancakes, 34
Pasta
  aubergine bolognese,
    41
  saucy ham pasta, 49
  vegetable lasagne, 40
Pastry
  cheesy shapes, 92
  fat cats, 13
  Marmite and cheese
    whirls, 93
  mini cheese and ham
    tarts, 31
Peanut butter
  shape sorters, 58
  sticky chicken, 14
Peas
  eggy bread
    butterflies, 60
  four fast fishes, 55
  shepherd's pie, 22
  tuna fish cakes, 23
Peppers
  aubergine bolognese,
    41

Mexican mince, 20
peppered beef
  casserole, 18
pick-up sticks, 32
quickie kebabs, 50
sandwich snails, 66
Pick-up sticks, 32
Pizza
  pizza clocks, 64
  shape sorters, 58
Plums
  jolly jellies, 74
Pork
  pork and lentil
    casserole, 29
  pork hot-pot, 28
  sticky ribs and apple
    slaw, 30
Potatoes
  cheesy fish pie, 24
  lamb stew, 19
  pork hot-pot, 28
  potato boats, 36
  potato, carrot and
    courgette rosti, 38
  shepherd's pie, 22
  tuna fish cakes, 23
  veggie burgers, 38

R
Raspberries
  peach melba dessert,
    71
  raspberry sorbet, 73
  strawberry ripple ice
    cream, 72
Rice
  sweet and sour
    chicken, 45
  tuna risotto, 56

S
Sausages
  cowboy bangers and
    beans, 26
  mini toad-in-the-
    hole, 26
  noughts and crosses,
    62
  quickie kebabs, 50
  sandwich snails, 66
  sausage log cabins, 56
  sausage wrappers, 50

speedy sausage rolls, 64
Shepherd's pie, 22
Shortbread shapes, 83
Skinny dippers, 44
Smoked haddock
    surprise haddock parcels, 25
Sorbet
    raspberry sorbet, 73
    summer fruit sorbet, 73
Spanish omelette, 48
Speedy chicken pie, 42
Spinach
    saucy spinach pancakes, 34
Sticky chicken, 14
Sticky ribs and apple slaw, 30
Strawberries
    cheat's trifle, 78
    strawberry ice cream, 72
    strawberry ripple ice cream, 72
    traffic light sundaes, 77
Surprise haddock parcels, 25
Sweet and sour chicken, 45
Sweetcorn
    aubergine bolognese, 41
    four fast fishes, 55
    sandwich snails, 66
    tuna fish cakes, 23

T

Tomatoes
    aubergine bolognese, 41
    ham and tomato scramble, 46
    pork and lentil casserole, 29
    quickie kebabs, 50
    vegetable lasagne, 40
Traffic light cakes, 85
Traffic light sundaes, 77
Trifle
    cheat's trifle, 78
Tuna
    tuna fish cakes, 23
    tuna flowers, 61
    tuna risotto, 56

V

Vegetables, 9
    fat cats, 37
    pick-up sticks, 32
    saucy ham pasta, 49
    tuna flowers, 61
    tuna risotto, 56
    vegetable lasagne, 40
    veggie burgers, 38

Y

Yogurt
    bananarama, 71
    cheat's trifle, 78
    jolly jellies, 74
    yogurt lollies, 74

Acknowledgements

The Department of Health; National Dairy Council Nutrition Service; Dr Nigel Dickie from Heinz Baby Foods; The British Dietetic Association; The Health Visitors' Association; Broadstone Communications for supplying the Kenwood equipment for recipe testing and photography; hand-painted china plates, bowls and mugs from Cosmo Place Studio Tel. 0171 278 3374; Tupperware for plain-coloured plastic bowls, plates, feeder beakers and cups; Cole and Mason for non-breakable children's ware; Royal Doulton for Bunnykins china; Spode for blue and white Edwardian Childhood china

MODELS

The publishers would like to thank the following children and adults for being such wonderful models: Maurice Bishop, Andrew Brown, Penny and Chloe Brown, Daisy May Bryant, April Cain, Helen and Matthew Coates, Cameron Gillis, Jamie Grant, Sandra and George Hadfield, Ted Howard, Emily Johnson, Huw and Rhees Jones, Key, Stephen, Charlie and Genevive Riddle, William Lewis, Sadé Walsh, Lionel and Lucy Watson, Lily May Whitfield, Philippa Wish, James Wyatt.